By the Shores of
❧ Lough Neagh ❧

Brian Cassells

BALLYHAY BOOKS

First published by Cottage Publications,
an imprint of Laurel Cottage Ltd.
Ballyhay, Donaghadee, N. Ireland 2008.
Copyrights Reserved.
© Text Brian Cassells 2008.
All rights reserved.
No part of this book may be reproduced or stored on any media
without the express written permission of the publishers.
Design & origination in N. Ireland.
Printed & bound in Portugal
ISBN 978 1 900935 71 5

For Maree, Julia and Lynn

Acknowledgements

I am hugely indebted to my sister Florence who made suggestions, gave endless encouragement and corrected the text. Many others have gone to great lengths to provide source material for this book; Michael Pollard who photocopied so much material, Ian Leinster who also provided advice and help, Stevie McElroy who was generous in donating me a book I will always treasure and to Caroline Marshall and Seamus Burns who provided resource material. To Brendan McAnallen of Benburb, someone who is a fount of knowledge and a delight to engage in conversation and to Margaret Clarke, who after a chance meeting sent me valuable background reading material.

Numerous others have inspired and helped me over the years, Dr Frank McCorry and Kieran Clendinning have been life long friends, Rev Ted Fleming, George Robinson sadly now deceased and my former history teacher Bill Crawford, who made me realise I was privileged to be born in a very special place, often derided, but secretly envied. The late Jim McGarry told me so much about the lough, how I wished I had listened more intently. I have been privileged to know some wonderful inspiring waterway writers as friends, Ruth Delany who has written numerous books on the Irish waterways always encouraged me to write and May Blair, a true lady who wrote the amazing book *Once upon the Lagan.* Also Brian Goggin who edited *Inland Waterways News.*

I have been involved with the local historical society for most of my life; the information I have gleaned has never failed to stimulate and fascinate me. My involvement with the Inland Waterways Association of Ireland who chose me as their leader and where I have sincere loyal friends, Michael, Drew, Con, John, Jim, Paddy, Victor, the list is endless. Thanks too to Mervyn King who has been invaluable as my IT adviser, to lifelong friends, Cyril, Sydney and Jim who kept encouraging me in many different ways, thanks lads. Michael Savage is a very special person, he is Mr Ram's Island, his dream is slowly becoming a reality, no matter what I ask Michael to do, it is achieved willingly and graciously, thank you Michael.

Writing a book requires enormous effort; the time taken is immeasurable, early morning to late at night for months and months, for me; well I was hidden away in my study at the back of the garage surrounded by books, books and more books, impaled in front of my computer. I feel I must pay tribute to my wife Maree, for endless patience, encouragement and cups of tea, for enduring solitary hour upon hour upon hour to allow me to write, write and write; it is quite a sacrifice, any success the book may have is partly yours too, thanks again. To daughters Julia and Lynn who although based in London would telephone asking, "How many words now, Dad?" Again, thanks for the encouragement to keep going.

All research and writing is not a chore, there are special moments and times when you re-engage with special friends that you have been privileged to meet along life's journey. Two such people are Ann Stevenson and her uncle, Jim Totten, a sprightly octogenarian. I spent a truly awesome morning with Jim and listened intently as he told me stories when as a child he swotted the cleggs off the horse's back during threshing. Ann and Jim are very special individuals who have a deep understanding of country people, especially those around the Tunny. I wish to also acknowledge the contribution of Victor Sefton, Bobbie Campbell and Betty McKee, Betty bakes delicious boiled cake, I know!

Many years ago while campaigning for the re-opening of the Ulster Canal I was privileged to meet the quiet gentleman, Jim Canning, a fount of knowledge on everything Coalisland. Jim graciously made available his extensive collection of old photographs of the South West Lough Neagh area, just listening to Jim's extensive knowledge is an inspiration to anyone.

Thanks to all who offered photographs. To illustrate the book with material from the past was a challenge, to Elaine and Paul in Craigavon Museum Service and to Charles Gardiner a local businessman who is another inspired individual with a love and detailed knowledge of his birthplace, thank you for your help. Thanks too are due to Ruth and John and the Morrow family and to Hilda Winter for photographs. Please forgive any omissions of thanks, I have gathered photographs over the years and I genuinely don't know where many came from.

While researching the text I met some wonderful lough shore people who were gracious in their welcome and generous with their knowledge. These are the people I grew up with, my people, they are justly proud of the lough shore, as I am; what a unique privilege to feel part of that identity. May I say to all, hold your head high, citizens who have been leaders in society, intellects of the highest order claim the lough shore as their birthplace and are rightly proud, sadly there are those who would mock and deride country people.

A special word of thanks to Tim Johnston of Cottage Publications and to his staff, especially Carolyn Scott for the design work. Tim is always positive and encouraging – when deadlines approach such attributes are appreciated. Jane Crosbie edited and polished my text, I have always felt it is impossible to correct your own work, thanks Jane for all your suggestions and help.

Contents

Overlooking Derryadd Bay

Where would you ever start a journey around such a vast lake often described as 'Ulster's Inland Sea'? Well for me that is obvious, start at home in Derryadd, a townland in the Montiaghs outside Lurgan in the South Lough Neagh wetlands, the place where I was born.

Home for me was a bungalow on a low hill overlooking Derryadd Bay, a modest home with a gigantic view. Much of the low lying wetland around Lough Neagh is now constituted as a Ramsar site, a wetland area of international importance. The South Lough Neagh Wetlands are a triangular area on the Southern shores of the lough, bounded on one side by the shoreline, on another by the Upper Bann River and by drawing a line from the town of Lurgan across to its neighbouring town, Portadown.

The view from our front door was spectacular, well that's what our visitors said, I guess we never really noticed it and certainly didn't appreciate it. We were within a stone's throw of the water's edge and on the horizon was a long low island, Croaghan, giving shelter to the bay. I say 'horizon' advisedly, for such a vast area of water has indeed a horizon. The lough is roughly thirty kilometres long and approximately twelve kilometres wide; for its size, it is relatively shallow – for most of its area, depths are no more than ten metres with the deepest part in the north east corner registering some thirty

metres. Much of the shoreline is not easily accessible by road and the entire lough deserves respect from any would be navigator. There are some six major inflowing rivers, the Blackwater and the Upper Bann on the southern end, the Ballinderry and the Moyola in the west, the Maine and the Six Mile Water to the north. Six make one, for the Lower Bann is the only out-flowing river.

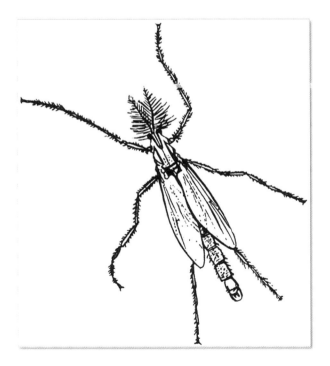

Chironomid Midge

A barge being towed across Lough Neagh

Anyone who visits the lough shore in May and early June cannot help but be affected by the Chironomid Midge, commonly known as the Lough Neagh fly. Those who live near the shore know never to open the windows and definitely never of an evening when the electric light is switched on. Despite their annoyance, they don't bite, but boy oh boy, they swarm! On a summer's evening there are huge black clouds of them and the humming sound is very noticeable. Allegedly they only live one or two days, spending their adult life mating and laying eggs for the cycle to begin again. Along the water's edge it is not uncommon to see huge amounts of these creatures, dead and decomposing in the water. Apparently they form an essential part of the food chain for wild life of the Neagh basin, but my memory of them is riding along on my bicycle when they got in my hair, up my nose and inside my shirt, oh well, at least they don't bite!

In the canal era, Lough Neagh was the hub of the waterway network for the Newry, Coalisland and Lagan canals with the Upper and Lower Bann navigations delivering the barges to the Lough Neagh basin. Over the years the shape and shoreline of the lough have changed as a number of flood alleviation schemes have lowered the level by over two metres. Sadly today the waters are quite badly polluted; indeed its status is described as hypertrophic, meaning the water has a high phosphorous content. Hopefully the future for water qual-

The old shoreline of Lough Neagh

ity is brighter; the European Water Framework Directive should ensure man has greater respect for this unique natural resource. The waters of the lough have for centuries provided a source of food from what was once a plentiful supply of fish and in the last century has provided for a thriving sand extraction industry. As well as the main source of drinking water for the province its waters were utilised by agriculture and in the linen industry.

The name Neagh is reputedly derived from Eochu, meaning the lake of the horse god. Many will be familiar with the mythological story of how Finn McCool scooped out a piece of earth thus creating the Lough Neagh basin, then threw it into the Irish Sea, hence the Isle of Man was created! I con-fess to liking the tale of the lady who, distracted by the cry of her child, had left the lid off a magic well where she had been drawing water, the well over flowed and created Lough Neagh. The geologists inform us that the lough was formed in tertiary times when the outpouring of basalt formed the Antrim Plateau. Earth movements accompanying these outpourings resulted in subsidence and the basin thus formed was filled with water. The water from the melting glaciers at the end of the last ice age some twenty thousand years ago meant the area of water then produced was much more extensive than the area of the present lake. Archaeologists claim to have found evidence of habitation in the Lough Neagh basin from the Stone Age era, more recently some suggest evidence of Viking raiders entering from the Lower Bann and penetrating up the Southern rivers, perhaps even led by Thorkils, the Viking king who ruled much of Ireland from his Lough Neagh fleets.

Lough Neagh is the largest fresh water lake in all of the British Isles and the third largest in Europe behind Lake Geneva and Lake Constance. The shoreline touches five of the six counties of Northern Ireland, Fermanagh being the outsider! Surprisingly it has only two large islands, Coney in the south and Ram's Island off the eastern shoreline. Those who have for centuries fished and sailed the waters know only too well how treacherous the waters can become, the waves are sharp and quick; sadly over the years it has claimed the lives of too many who ventured on its waters.

Much of the land around the lough is low lying and the shoreline is often reedy and marshy. In wintertime rainfall levels are higher and this of-

ten results in flooding, as a result of which, down through the centuries, this flooding has created peat bogs though these are more prolific in the south and south-west. The north-eastern corner boasts deposits of diatomite previously used in the manufacture of pottery. The lough is now recognised as one of the most important areas for migrating birds and areas like Oxford Island, Lough Beg and sites along the western shore are of international importance.

Manufacturing opportunities are largely concentrated along the northern, eastern and southern shores although this constitutes less than one quarter of job occupations; agriculture would be by far the largest employer in the Lough Neagh basin. The western shore is a much more isolated rural area with fewer job opportunities and in the nineteenth century experienced high levels of emigration.

In the book *The Way That I Went* by Robert Louis Praeger (published in 1937), Praeger talks of the 'Water Guns' of Lough Neagh, a strange booming noise accompanying a whirl wind, like a sort of modern twister, heard always in the daytime. When talking to older fishermen many admit to knowing of the phenomenon, though all seem to have heard this in the distance and strangely they have all experienced this on calm days and never experienced any water disturbance. John Wesley on one of his many trips to the area talked of the magical powers the waters possessed and how they could turn wood to stone, certainly even today ex-

The Great Crested Grebe

Bluebells, with the round tower in the background, Coney Island

amples of this petrified wood abound along the shoreline.

The following is the second verse of a poem by Thomas Moore, called *Let Erin Remember,* which to me aptly describes these beautiful, magical waters.

On Lough Neagh's banks as the fisherman strays
In the clear cold eve declining
He sees the round towers of other days
In the waters 'neath him shining
Thus shall memory often in dreams sublime
Catch a glimpse of the days that are over
Thus sighing, look through the waves of time
For the long-faded glories they cover.

13

The sluice gates at Toome in the foreground

The bed and soil of Lough Neagh is owned and administered by the Shaftesbury estates, a throw back to the Plantation of Ulster. They gained a considerable amount of additional land as a result of the lowering of levels on a number of occasions over the years. The original title to Lough Neagh was granted by Charles I to the Earl of Donegal and then transferred to the Chichester family and eventually to the estate of Lord Shaftesbury. The asset brings in substantial revenue as ownership includes the shooting rights, mineral rights to extract sand and gravel, and rights for laying moorings and building jet-

ties. The estate does not claim navigation rights or to own the water. The recent sudden death of two members of the Shaftesbury family mean substantial death duties will now be required to be paid; this has given rise to concern as to the future ownership.

The lough is aligned in a north south direction and is almost rectangular in shape. The western shore is much more rural in character, really due to the fact there are fewer main centres of population. There have been four lowerings of the lough over the years, from the McMahon scheme of 1847 to 1858, Shepherd's from 1932 to 1942 with two further schemes in 1952 and 1959. Thus today's shoreline is quite different to that which originally existed. Evidence of the original shoreline abounds, evidenced by a high bank and, where left to nature, the alder tends to dominate tree growth. Since time immemorial it has been seen as an asset and as a barrier; it provided a means of transport for the early settler and yet is a barrier between east and west. In the past before the lowering, flooding was always a problem, however today levels are managed by sluices at Toome and on the Lower Bann.

Coney Island on the southern shore is one of the two larger islands; it guards the entrance to the mouths of the River Blackwater and of the Upper Bann. The island lies approximately one kilome-

MAGHERAFELT · TOOME
· RANDALSTOWN
BALLYRONAN · ANTRIM

LOUGH CRUMLIN
ARDBOE · NEAGH
GLENAVY
STEWARTSTOWN
COALISLAND LISBURN
CLONOE

LURGAN

· PORTADOWN

Coney Island

tre from the shore of the townland of Maghery. Evidence existed of a wooden planked causeway mounted on stakes from the townland of Derrywarragh over to the island, this has long since disappeared and was known locally as St Patrick's roadway. In spring the island is carpeted with bluebells and the nests of the herons, high up in the trees, present quite a spectacular tree top sight. Now covered with mature native trees, Coney was described in 1837 as having a few shrubs and some low trees. In the ordnance survey memoirs of 1835-8 it is suggested Coney derives its name from the number of rabbits that frequented the island.

The island shows considerable factual evidence of habitation from past times, boasting human habitation from as early as 6000 BC or 8000 years ago. The 13th century Anglo Norman motte, reputed to be the most westerly Norman outpost in these islands, and the remains of a 16th century round tower referred to as O'Neill's tower, provide a fascinating insight into a rich and varied past. Shane O'Neill, the famous Irish chieftain, used Coney as a secure keep for his accumulated treasures before Lord Sydney, the English Deputy, took them to England after O'Neill's death in 1567. Indeed on John Speede's map of 1610 the island was named Sidney Island and Lough Neagh was renamed

Cottage on Coney Island

Lough Sidney – thankfully the name didn't survive. In Victorian times, Coney Island was in the ownership of Lord Charlemont who built a delightful summer cottage which has been tastefully restored by the National Trust. The cottage was built in 1895 by James Alfred Caulfield, VII Viscount and XI Baron of Charlemont. He is reputably buried along with his horse within the wall of the round tower. More recently, locals will tell you stories of illicit stills brewing poteen on the island, and certainly Coney would have been an ideal location for such a venture, not exactly under the immediate gaze of the law. In the iron-age era the island site was used to smelt iron ore from the Sperrin Mountains. The island today is owned by the National Trust and managed by Craigavon Borough Council. The ever welcoming warden, Peter McClelland gives a fascinating insight into the history and wild life of the island; it is well worth a visit.

Ram's Island lies mid-way down the eastern shore lying across Lennymore Bay; it was mentioned in the *Annals of the Four Masters,* one of the earliest written records. The island is approximately one mile long by a quarter of a mile wide. A round tower is situated behind the roofless building that was once the summer house of Lord O'Neill.

Line drawing of cottage on Ram's Island

Pictures still remain of this charming building, the church like windows and arched doorway complemented the wide over-hanging thatched roof. It was originally dashed with reddish coloured pebbles, most of which have been lost due to the effects of the weather – now only the handmade red brick is visible. The remains of a second much smaller house are much more difficult to trace; it is at the other end of the island, being the residence of the Cardwell family who looked after the island for the O'Neills.

The origin of the island's name is shrouded in speculation; on Speede's map of 1610 it was recorded as 'Enis Garden' and this map shows the symbol of a church tower. Local tradition states that the ruins of an old church were still clearly visible in the middle of the eighteenth century and human bones, including several complete skeletons, were discovered close to the tower as

were brass pins and a coin of Edward I. The tower is intriguing, the doorway being over two metres from the ground and two small interestingly shaped windows. In the early nineteenth century the island was owned by a local fisherman called David McAreavey who sold it to the O'Neills for the grand sum of one hundred guineas. At that time the area was in the region of six acres, with the lough lowering this has now grown to approximately forty acres. Around the original shoreline large stones protected the bank, beautifully laid and carefully paved despite their vast size.

The story of the Cardwell family was superbly recorded by the late Jim McGarry, a true gentleman whom I was privileged to know. What Jim and the McGarry family didn't know about the lough wasn't worth knowing. He vividly describes Robert and Jane Cardwell in most eloquent lan-

Robert and Jane Cardwell

guage, talking about their self-sufficient existence on the island with only a monthly trip to the shop at Rose's Lane Ends where they purchased that which was necessary to supplement their organic lifestyle. Jane was gardener, keeper of the O'Neill cottage, baker and cook with an amazing number of traditional craft skills while Robert was fisherman, boatman, handyman and communicator with the outside world. Jane wore long clothes, a traditional shawl, high sided boots and a bonnet, her personality endeared her to all who were privileged to come into her company. Robert was smaller, stockily built and immensely strong. There were many visitors especially in summer who came to enjoy a picnic in the awesome yet serene surroundings, to enjoy Jane's array of flowers and chat to these inspired custodians who were at one with nature. Robert passed away in 1929 in his late nineties; Jane followed him three years later, she was aged one hundred and two. The likes of her funeral was rarely seen even then. Eight Lough Neagh fishing boats in an orderly row formed the funeral cortege, a tribute to one who lived a unique life by any standards. The Cardwells were truly Lough Neagh folk, no stress in their life, just work, hard work and lots of it, time was unimportant, the job had to be done and it was done to the very best of their ability.

The late Jim McGarry's dream of making the island once again accessible was to be taken up by Michael Savage and members of a branch of the Inland Waterways Association of Ireland, the River Bann and Lough Neagh Association. Lord

Funeral cortege for Jane Cardwell

O'Neill caught the vision and generously leased the island for a nominal rent. Funding was sought and obtained to create a unique natural experience, to open up the island to visitors. Nowadays a ferryboat *The Island Warrior* takes visitors to explore the island, contact details are on the web site www.ramsisland.org. Landing on the island is at a new modern jetty where an old John Kelly coal barge is to be moored. This is being refurbished as an interpretation centre with an interpretive area, kitchen and toilet facilities. The newly created paths and wooden steps convey the visitor to the higher ridge of the island where they may wander and enjoy the wild flowers that abound in season. Hopefully the former O'Neill cottage, burned during the last war, will one day be restored to its former glory; that indeed would be a fitting finale to Jim McGarry's vision.

Lough shore folk are unique, that is without question. Throughout history when our land was ravaged by famine and pestilence, fresh water fish provided a staple diet for those with the ability to harvest its crop. Studies throughout the famine

Trowagh Bay, now more commonly known as the Bay Shore

era of the mid 1800s illustrate significant higher survival rates in shore-based townlands. However any water-based activity brings risk and folklore and many place names around the lough will testify to tragedies of past days. For example, Trowagh Bay on the southern shores, now more commonly referred to as the Bay Shore, roughly translated from the Irish means Bay of sorrows, a reminder of some long forgotten tragedy that afflicted the local populace.

Centuries of fishing on the lough have left us with unique names for shallow and deep areas, names such as Old Bog Hole, Nanny's Mud, White Horse Flat and Joker Flat, which conjure up images perceived by local fishermen. As a child when allowed to swim on sultry summer days, I vividly recall being warned not to venture out too far as I might go over the edge into deep water known as The Gut. Many of these holes were caused by the sand dredgers; I also recall catching pike on a spinner where these deep areas came close to the shore. Croaghan island lay in the bay in front of where I lived, it was off Roughlan point; to a small boy it looked huge, sadly now I know it to be of modest size and other than a breeding ground and a hide for wild fowlers is relatively unimportant. In 1947 during an exceptionally severe winter the waters of the lough froze for some considerable distance out from the shore and some family members walked from Derryadd bay to Croaghan Island.

This cradle of Mid Ulster is littered with historical artefacts, castles, raths, forts, ancient church-

Lough Neagh fishing boat

es, graveyards and estates, examples abound. Here too much of the history of the island of Ireland was enacted, the Battle of Benburb, the Flight of the Earls, the estate known as Shane's castle, Massereene's castle and gardens at Antrim and the ecclesiastical sites that litter the shoreline. All events are inter-linked in some strange way, complex yet interdependent, evolving to explain our crazy sectarian mistrust, Protestant, Catholic and Dissenter, not to mention everyone else!

It often seems to me that historians have endeavoured to simplify our past; I ask myself the question, is that really possible, am I foolish to even try, indeed, do I fully understand this labyrinth that we refer to as the history of Ireland and especially that of the province of Ulster. It must be

seen as that of pre-1600 when the native Irish were largely in control and that of post-1600 when the English finally conquered Ulster, this is the era we refer to as the Plantation. We are all well aware of the conflict of 1690; I'm not for one minute suggesting we understand the true facts, rather, in this era sometimes I think we choose what we want to believe!

Vast Lough Neagh

The People of the Lough Shore 2

For those who have sailed Lough Neagh, this is a large stretch of water that deserves ultimate respect. Conditions may change abruptly and often the morning that starts calm, peaceful and serene may end uninviting with angry clouds, turbulent waters and poor visibility. Because of the nature of the low shoreline, recognisable land marks may be difficult to distinguish. Rain brings misty conditions and for those unfamiliar with the topography, this can be an inclement, lonely spot – is it any wonder that it is described as Ulster's Inland Sea?

All too often adversity is recorded in poetic verse such as the Green family tragedy of August 1904 when the yacht *Osprey* capsized off Ardmore Point claiming six young lives: Frank, aged 19, Dorothy, aged 16, their two Belfast cousins, John, aged 21, and Herbert, aged 19, along with two school friends from Guernsey, Hugh Catchpool, aged 19, and Frank Catchpool, aged 18. Winifred Green, aged 22, was the sole survivor. Interestingly even today, the tragedy still has the ability to shock such was the enormity of the loss of fragile youthful life.

The emotion inspired by this explicit verse written by S. L. McFarland cannot fail to recreate the shock felt in the area, a stark reminder even today of the respect the waters of the lough deserve.

The Hand of cruel death has come and cast a cloudy gloom,
Six persons without warning have been hurried to the tomb.
Three homes are plunged in grief today, sorrow hard to bear,
Two from each home by untimely death, are called from earthly care.

From Kinnego, near Lurgan town, five boys and two girls,
Set sail for Coney Island, not thinking of their peril,
But while returning on that fateful night, a gale on the Lough did rise
And suddenly without warning the 'Osprey' did capsize.

For a while to the keel of the upturned boat the party all did hold,
But two of the boys named Catchpool were soon benumbed with cold,
They could no longer hold for life and both of them let go,
And sank into the waters dark and died in the depths below.

A boy called Frank Green suggested then, that he would swim to land
And call for help while the rest remained, but death was near at hand
As he started on his perilous errand the yacht's bow struck his head
And he sank into the depths below and very soon was dead.

His cousins John and Herbert soon could not bear the strains,
And both of them relaxed their grip, and for days weren't seen again,
The ladies still did bravely cling to the keel of the upturned boat,
And struggled hard for precious life, as it from the scene did float.

For a while Miss Winifred, boldly swam supporting her sister dear,
Then Dorothy swam awhile herself, but death it soon drew near.
And Miss Winifred when near the land was soon to be alone,
For Dorothy got exhausted and death claimed her for its own.

Miss Winifred did all she could to save her sister's life,
But death the 'Warrior' conquered in that sad and painful strife,
The Heroine then swam to land and went to a farmer's house,
But fainted before she was able the sad news to make known.

When consciousness returned to her, she told the awful tale,
How all her companions had been drowned in that returning sail,
And early in the morning to her home she was conveyed,
When the story once again was told by that heroic Maid.

The bodies weren't found all at once, nine days did pass away,
Ere the remaining two were taken from the waters of Lough Neagh.
And many people mourned those days, as they beheld each sight,
The victims of the tragedy on that sad Tuesday night.

And many eyes were wet with tears as onward to the tomb,
The hearses bore their bodies that now are wrapped with gloom
Lord bless their parents in their grief and sooth them each and all
Bless all who now are sorely tried by the sad and sullen call.

Ferries enabling locals and livestock to get across rivers were an important means of communication; Maghery had one such ferry across the Blackwater and I can recall the remains of a crude platform lying in the Maghery canal, so I assume its demise was somewhere towards the latter end of the twentieth century. The Blackwater ferry was similar to the Bannfoot ferry which operated up until the early 1980s. It was operated by the Wilson family for generations, latterly by Willie who was bent and stooped with age. Vehicles would hoot the horn to summon Willie from the adjoining house; donning his cap, Willie would walk the short distance and proceed to untie the platform. With short pulls he would feed the rope tied across the river to a post on each bank through his hands and gradually ease the ferry across. Willie never refused help, especially when the river was in flow and the ferry angled; from

The Bannfoot ferry

the bank the square shape became a diamond but I never heard of a mishap. Once there were three ferries operating on the Upper Bann, local politicians called for bridges, indeed still do, however the only bridge I ever recall was an army exercise when a bailey bridge was erected across the river. There were ferries too on the Lower Bann, probably the best known was a chain ferry at Newferry near Toome and there was a ferry which operated at Portglenone before the building of the bridge.

Other than Antrim, few of the main centres of population are actually close to the water's edge; nevertheless, the lough has influenced the development of most centres of population, big and small. Larger towns such as Lurgan, Portadown, Dungannon, Magherafelt, Antrim and Lisburn

have benefited from their proximity to Lough Neagh as have the smaller areas such as Coalisland, Stewartstown, Ardboe, Ballyronan, Glenavy, Crumlin and Ballinderry.

The history of the town of Lurgan goes back to the early 1600s and the plantation of Ulster. Before that time the population of the area was dominated by the McCann family, although the area they cultivated and where they actually lived is a matter of conjecture. In fact pre-plantation, the whole of the south Lough Neagh area was in the McCann family possession. One of the earliest maps of the area, with a date of 1609 lists the townlands and shows a roofless church in Shankill, meaning old church. The study of townlands and the derivation of their names is a fascinating subject, already there are a number of excellent books written on this subject. The lands around Lurgan were granted to a distinguished English family from Nottingham, the Brownlows, who established a settlement which was the beginnings of the town of Lurgan. Typically English, the town has a wide main street that originally had a middle row. The initial years were turbulent for the fledgling settlement but Brownlow persisted and the town grew in size. Over the years the land bank grew, indeed by the early 1700s estates were added in Louth, Armagh and Monaghan.

Today the town still boasts the former residence of the Brownlow family known locally as Brownlow House, the second such dwelling on this site. This grand ornate Elizabethan manor house was designed by the celebrated Edinburgh architect, William Playfair and originally stood in a demesne of three hundred acres and also boasted a fine sheet of water frequented by a rich variety of wild fowl. The ornate grounds were largely to the front of the house. The family were popular landlords, well respected by all classes and creeds and represented the area as members of parliament for numerous years, it is suggested Arthur was the only member of parliament at the end of the seventeenth century, to sit in both the James II and the William & Mary Parliaments – it could be suggested he had a foot in both camps! In the early nineteenth century Charles Brownlow was elevated to the peerage, indeed the title of Lord Lurgan existed until virtually the end of the twentieth century when the lineage finally ceased. The end of the nineteenth century saw the demise of the family locally – eventually house and grounds were separated; the house was sold and the garden and the man-made lake now form the beautiful Lurgan Park, without doubt one of the finest in Ireland.

The Brownlow family were well known for their interest in coursing their most famous greyhound being Master McGrath, a greyhound initially described as the runt of the litter that went on to win the Waterloo Cup, the most prestigious award of the coursing world, no less than three times. The dog was allegedly rescued by a young helper called McGrath and trained by a Mr Walsh, and the dog is still talked about in the town even today although the following poem, *The Ballad of Master McGrath,* tells the story far better than I could ever relate it.

Eighteen sixty-nine was the date of the year,
The Waterloo sportsmen and more did appear,
For to gain a great prize, and to bear it awa'
With the Champion of England against "Master M'Gra"

On the 12th December, that day of renown,
M'Gra and his keeper they left Lurgan town,
A gale on the channel it soon drove them o'er,
On the 13th they landed on Fair England's shore.

And when they arrived in big London town;
The great English sportsmen they all gathered round,
And one of the gentlemen gave a "Ha-ha,"
Saying "Is that the great dog you call Master M'Gra?"

Then one of the gentlemen standing around,
Said what about you or your Irish greyhound,
For you or your greyhound we don't give a straw,
And we'll humble the pride of your "Master M'Gra."

Lord Lurgan stepped forward, and said, "Gentlemen,
If there's any amongst you has money to spend.
For your nobles of England I don't give a straw,
Here's five thousand to one upon "Master M'Gra."

Then "M'Gra" he looked up and wagged his big tail
Informing his Lordship I know what you mane,
But noble Brownlow don't fear them, ava.
For I'll tarnish their laurels, said "Master M'Gra."

Then Rose stood uncovered, the great English Pride,
The master and keeper they stood by her side,
The hare was left off, and the crowd did "Hurrah"
There's the pride of all England against "Master McGra."

As "Rose" and the "Master" they both ran along,
"Now I wonder," said Rose, "what brought you from home
You should have stopped there in your Irish demesne,
And not come to gain laurels on Albion's plain.

Well, I know," said M'Gra, "we have wild Irish bogs,
But you'll find in ould Ireland, there's good men and dogs;
Lead on, bold Britannia, give non of your jaw
"Snuff that up your nostrils," said Master McGra.

Lord Lurgan with Master McGrath

The hare she went off just as swift as the wind,
He was sometimes before her and sometimes behind;
Rose gave the first turn, according to law
But the second was given by Master McGra.

Then the hare she led on with a beautiful view,
And swift as the wind o'er the green field she flew;
But he jumped on her back, and held up his paw,
"Three cheers for ould Ireland," said Master M'Gra.

Lord Lurgan's second Quaker meeting house, built in 1881

The recent past saw the town of Lurgan as the centre of Ulster linen manufacture, the adjoining village of Waringstown being the home of cambric linen introduced by the Waring family and developed by Huguenot refugees from the North of France.

Lurgan boasts the oldest Quaker Meeting House in Ireland – the Religious Society of Friends were founded here in 1654. James Logan was born in the town in 1674 in Queen Street close to the site of the present meeting house. His father, a clergyman, had left the Church of Scotland and become a Quaker. To avoid possible persecution he had left Scotland to settle in Ulster, taking up employment as a schoolteacher in the Lurgan meetinghouse. At the tender age of thirteen the young James became apprenticed to a Dublin merchant, certainly not much time devoted to growing up; after a year he was forced to return home as James II's arrival created an unsettled situation throughout Ireland which forced the Logans to return to

Scotland. Before his seventeenth birthday he was offered a job teaching in Bristol, where he stayed for nearly three years. He wanted to emigrate to Jamaica but on returning home, his mother who had by this stage lost seven of her children, persuaded him against the idea. Early in 1699 William Penn, a family friend offered him a job as his secretary. Before the age of twenty five James set sail for America eventually becoming secretary to the governor Penn. Lurgan's unhappy boyhood blossomed into a highly respected intelligent government official who did much for the establishment of the state of Pennsylvania. Reputed to be fluent in thirteen languages including Arabic, he is remembered in his native Queen Street by an Ulster History Circle blue plaque.

George William Russell, a true intellectual, a writer, poet and radical thinker, was born in Lurgan on 10th April 1867. He spent his first eleven formative years in the town often returning to holiday in the townland of Drumgor. He was baptised in Shankill Parish Church and his primary education was received in Lurgan Model School before he and the family moved south to Dublin. Recently Russell was honoured by the Ulster History Circle when they erected a blue plaque on his former home in William Street to perpetuate the memory of Lurgan's world famous literary and artistic son. Russell was the son of a bookkeeper who was employed in a local linen factory. He was described as a mystic, artist and writer. A contemporary of W. B. Yeats and James Joyce, he started employment as a draper's clerk where he worked for six

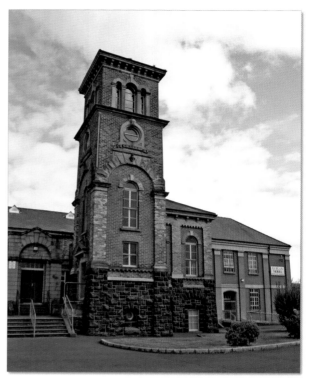

Lurgan Model Primary School

years, then he worked for the Irish Agricultural Organization Society which was an agricultural co-operative movement, where he helped establish a co-operative bank and credit societies. It was his success as a writer and painter that brought him world-wide fame; his writing career was launched as editor of *The Irish Homestead* moving eventually to *The Irish Statesman* using the pseudonym A. E. Russell published an enormous amount of poetry and his many paintings hang in many of

Statue commemorating Field Marshall Sir John Dill

the leading art galleries. Once described as a moderate Nationalist, Russell was a pacifist, a reformer, an encourager with an enormous humour and a deep love of Irish theatre. He counted among his friends, W. B. Yeats, Oscar Wilde, Lady Gregory, Patrick Kavanagh and Frank O'Connor to name but a few, and he was deeply involved with the Abbey Theatre. Oh that Russell's inspirational message in the following quotation was taken to heart today. *'We may fight against what is wrong, but*

if we allow ourselves to hate, that is to insure our spiritual defeat and our likeness to what we hate.'

While Russell may have been a pacifist, the town boasts the birth place of an important war strategist, Field Marshall Sir John Dill. Born in Market Street in December 1881, the son of a local bank manager Dill joined the first battalion of the Leinster Regiment and initially saw service in the Boer War. By the end of the First World War he had attained the rank of Brigadier General and had a reputation as an inspirational leader. Eventually rising to the rank of Chief of the Imperial General Staff during the Second World War, he found it difficult to work alongside Sir Winston Churchill and was eventually posted to Washington where his talents were recognised and appreciated. Dill died in Washington and is buried in Arlington State Cemetery where an equestrian statue, unveiled by Harry S. Trueman, perpetuates his memory.

The story of Sir Robert Hart is one to enthral any young boy. Born in Portadown, the son of a devout Methodist and educated in Queen's University, he became Inspector General of Foreign Customs in China. I can't really imagine many of the young lads from Portadown in the 1850s firstly heading off to work in Hong Kong, settling a dispute between the Portuguese and Chinese, and eventually having a street named after him in Beijing. To say he was highly respected is an understatement. His advice to the Chinese government led to the improvement and success of China's ports; he was

renowned for his managerial and diplomatic skills and was honoured by both Britain and China with numerous awards. After his retirement he became Pro Chancellor of Queen's University in Belfast. He is buried near the home to where he retired in Great Marlowe in Buckinghamshire in a graveyard opposite the River Thames.

I have always felt the town of Dungannon, while convenient to the lough, never really seemed to identify with the water as other towns closer to the shore did, perhaps this is only my perception, though I don't think I'm far wrong. The town today is a bustling thriving area; the new Linen Green centre on the outskirts has breathed new life into this former traditional linen factory and

is drawing shoppers to the area from the rest of the province. I have a good friend who constantly reminds me, he attended the Royal School in Dungannon, one of the five Royal Schools established in Ulster in 1608 and now celebrating over four hundred years providing quality education for South Tyrone. Inextricably linked with the history of Dungannon and the 'Flight of the Earls' with the subsequent 'Plantation of Ulster' the Royal Schools were founded by James I (VI Scotland) who decreed *'that there should be one free school, at least, appointed in every county, for the education of youths in learning and religion'.*

Hugh O'Neill, arguably the most powerful clan leader had fled Ireland, his castle in Dungannon

The old bridge over Six Mile Water near Clotworthy House

eighteen years in a Paris prison rather than hand over vast sums of money to those who had conned him, married two women he met while incarcerated, yet was unswerving in his loyalty to King and to Britain.

Clotworthy was indeed a grand house in every sense of the word, its loss cannot be underestimated. Within the walls were kept prized possessions two of which were the mace and the speaker's chair from the Irish House of Commons, the parliament before partition. The furniture was elaborately hand carved Irish oak no doubt utilising natural resources from the vast tree stock within the park. Hanging in the heavily panelled Oak Room, where three windows overlooked the river, were mirrors which dispersed the light around this otherwise dark room, here also to enhance the mystery was a secret spring that revealed a curious recess. The oak room housed other priceless treasures, huge canvas family portraits, fifteen heraldic shields depicting the coats of arms of the various speakers of the Irish Parliament and priceless books which included Archbishop Cranmer's New Testament which had been a gift from the Cranmer family and rare manuscripts relating to the Plantation of Ulster.

Northern Ireland's domestic airport has traditionally been associated with the village of Crumlin. Originally at Nutt's Corner and now at Aldergrove, Belfast International Airport is midway between Crumlin and Antrim. Driving through the village of Crumlin I am always con-

The Cockle House in Crumlin Glen

scious of the criss crossed iron railway bridge with quite a long span, the untidy remains of a former linen factory and the Pakenham Arms giving clues to the past history. The name Crumlin means 'crooked glen' perhaps derived from its position within the Crumlin river valley. Pakenham is the family that lived on the adjoining estate, part of which is now the Talnotry Cottage Bird Garden, which has sizable collections of partridge, pheasant and quail. Part of the estate is now a public pathway along the Crumlin glen; here you will find the 'Cockle House' overlooking the waterfall, allegedly built for an Arab Moslem servant who wished for a quiet place to pray, hence one of the windows faces east towards Mecca. The clock tower and weather vane in the centre of the town were erected in 1897 to the memory of Reverend Arthur Pakenham, who lived in the adjoining estate. Crumlin old church, referred to locally as the Abbey, dates from the thirteenth century and was destroyed in 1689 during the retreat of James from Londonderry. For the historian, look out for the ruins of Camlin old church, first recorded in 1306 and to be found to the north of Crumlin close to the river. Roger de Courcy is reputed to have had a castle here in 1218 called the Crooked Castle of Camlin, a name most likely a mispronunciation of Crumlin.

Crumlin sadly seems to be sitting still – the main street has a tired look though the coffee shop is well worth a visit if even to sample the delightful pastry! Here is a sleepy village in urgent need of sympathetic inspiration to enable it to rediscover itself and take its rightful place so close to Northern Ireland's main gateway.

Glenavy is a pretty village that nestles comfortably within the valley of the Glenavy River. According to tradition, St Patrick established a church here and eventually left one of his disciples, a man called Daniel who was small in stature; a more polite way of saying he was a dwarf, hence the derivation of the name is 'Church of the Dwarf'. Within the graveyard of St Aidan's Church of Ireland, there is a Bullaun stone, similar to those found in La Lou graveyard at Lower Ballinderry. There is confusion as to whether these were baptismal fonts or merely for grinding corn. Personally the fact they are found on ecclesiastical sites suggests to me the baptismal theory as the more likely solution. I like the unusual roof line of the houses on either side of the street, the village has retained the character of its main street, the locals have an obvious civic pride. One of Glenavy's proud sons is John Ballance who emigrated in 1866 from Ballypitmave, a townland just outside the village, to New Zealand where he formed the Liberal Party and eventually became prime minister in 1891; the original farm house still stands and is open at certain times to the public.

Many will have heard the humorous story of the gentleman from Ballinderry wanting to travel to visit a friend who lived in Peking in China and who hoped to make the journey by public transport. Going into the local railway station he inquired of the ticket collector the price of a sin-

Bullaun Stone in La Lou Graveyard

gle ticket to Peking. The collector advised that he would only be able to issue a ticket as far as Belfast and that he should inquire there at the ticket office. The story continues and the gent is further advised he must proceed to London to obtain such a ticket. Eventually he arrived, enjoyed the holiday and it was time to return. Making his way to the railway station he went up to the ticket desk and inquired if he could purchase a single ticket to Ballinderry. The Chinese gentleman replied asking, "Is it Upper or Lower Ballinderry you wish to travel to Sir?"

Ballinderry, much heralded in the song, *Tis pretty to be in Ballinderry* means the town of the Oakwood. Arriving at Upper Ballinderry today, the building that attracts the eye is the antique and china shop, this fine three storey building was built in

SIX FOOT OPPOSITE LYES THE
BODY OF LOUIS CROMMELIN
BORN AT ST. QUENTIN FRANCE
ONLY SON TO LOUIS CROMM-
ELIN AND ANN CROMMELIN
DIRECTOR OF THE LINEN MAN-
UFACTORY WHO DIED BELOVED
OF ALL AGED 28 YEARS THE 1ST OF
JULY 1711
SISTE VIATOR ET UT ILLE DUM VITA
MANNEBAT SUSPICE COELUM DES-
PICE MUNDUM ET RESPICE FINEM
ALSO THE BODY OF MARY MAD-
ELIENE BERNIERE WIFE OF
CAPTAIN BERNIERE ONLY DAUGH-
TER OF LEWIS CROMMELIN
DECEASED THE 8th OF JULY 1715
AGED 21 YEARS
HERE ALSO LYETH THE REMAINS OF
LOUIS CROMMELIN SENR WHO
DIED 7th JULY 1727 AGED 75 YEARS
ALSO THE BODY OF ANNE WIFE
OF LOUIS CROMMELIN DECEAS-
ED THE 15th AUGUST 1755 AGED
97 YEARS

The grave of Louis Crommelin

the early 1700s and was originally a staging post on the road to Dublin, though has also seen service as a grain store and a bicycle shop. Today lots of people want to live in this area, evidenced by the large numbers of new houses built in recent years. This is an area steeped in history, the important ecclesiastical settlements, the huge estate that was Lord Conway's, the massive oak forest with the adjoining deer park which stretched from Lisburn to Lough Neagh. The first Lord Conway, Edward lived in Lisburn in the area now known as Castle Gardens and his rural retreat was the castle at Portmore. Sir George Rawdon who lived in Moira was his brother-in-law and the two men did much to improve living conditions for their tenants. Lower Ballinderry, lower that is to the lough, like Upper is situated on a crossroads, the cream walled Moravian church sits comfortably with other seventeenth century buildings creating a peaceful scene that hasn't changed much over the years. Nearby on the road to Upper Ballinderry stands an imposing old two storey dwelling, Ballinderry House and on the front wall is a plaque recording the visit of John Wesley on 5th July 1771 where he preached from an upstairs window to a large crowd that had gathered around the house.

The lands around Portmore Lough, virtually a complete circle, are now a nature reserve situated within the townland of Portmore, the area deserves special mention. Remember here was the deer park and the great oak wood of Lord Conway's estate. A story survives of a tree blown down around 1760 that had a circumference of over forty feet. Allegedly when planked, the wood was used to build a barge or as it was better known, a Lough Neagh lighter as well as many items of furniture, I wonder do any survive today? Portmore Castle was a building of some note, a very imposing edifice. Taxation at that time was based on hearths and it is recorded in 1669 as having eighteen hearths, much marble, and stables where water was piped

Lisburn, around a century ago

to the horse's head. Today the extensive stone wall is all that remains of this once magnificent dwelling dismantled in the eighteenth century when all that remained was sold off.

The council area of the city of Lisburn touches the shores of the lough in this area. I must acknowledge the superb work that has been undertaken in Lisburn to recreate the tiered walls that step down towards the river Lagan. This was the home of Sir Fluke Conway, an officer of the English army who, with the demise of the O'Neills, had acquired the land, known then as Lisnagarvey and settled it with English and Welsh settlers. The name changed some sixty years later – many explanations have been proffered, I shall here again avoid controversy and simply continue! The

Duke of Schomberg, on his way to what would be known as the Battle of the Boyne, is reputed to have stayed in the house where Bishop Jeremy Taylor had resided at 13 Castle Street and William Prince of Orange dined in a house at the corner of Market Street. Mind you I'm tempted to say if these two gentlemen stayed and dined everywhere that they are alluded to, then it is little wonder it took them so long to reach Drogheda! William must have been influenced by someone in the area as eventually he removed the tax on linen, hence the growth of this thriving industry in the mid Ulster area. This was contrary to other taxes which forbade other exports that could have threatened the English economy.

In 1698 a French Huguenot refugee called Louis

Crommelin with his son, also called Louis, arrived in Lisburn with a company of about seventy people, few of whom spoke any English, having been forced to leave Northern France because of religious persecution by Louis XIV. Three years later Crommelin established a bleaching factory at Hilden conveniently beside the river and eventually creating a port on the Lagan navigation. Interestingly French Huguenot names survive to this very day – names such as Dupre, Dubourdieu and Goyer are found in various parts of Northern Ireland. It is fair to say Crommelin standardised the weaving process and as production increased disaster struck. A huge fire in 1707 destroyed the primitive settlement that was Lisburn, including the castle and the Cathedral, and sadly the castle was never rebuilt. Many of the immigrants scattered to the surrounding villages, some returned to their homeland, thankfully some remained to rebuild what we recognise today as the basis for the modern city of Lisburn. Lisburn is a river town, straddling the river Lagan and much of its success may be attributable to the fact it was the main port between Belfast and Lough Neagh. At a stage there were nine quays operational on the Lagan canal in Lisburn; here too was the dry dock, the 'garage' for the Lagan lighters. Nearby is the Maze race course, which was established by William Hill of Hillsborough in 1744, a slight hill in the centre of the course afforded spectators a view of the pro-

All that remains of Magheranagaw Old Church

ceedings. According to legend and folklore Saint Patrick visited Crew Hill, as did the High King of all Ireland, Brian Boru. The rath and earthworks are still discernible just off the Glenavy Road out of Lisburn.

Recently I read a fascinating book by Anthony S. Drennan on Laura Bell. Allegedly she was born in Glenavy, became a prostitute in Belfast, later graduating to being a courtesan of nineteenth century Dublin and London and, among other amorous skirmishes, had a romantic affair with a Nepalese Prince which led to the formation of the Ghurkha regiment and finally ending up as a lay preacher to poor tenant Scottish farmers. How about that for

a varied and interesting life!

Harold George Ferguson, better known as Harry Ferguson, was born in April 1884 outside Dromore, not exactly Lisburn but I suppose near enough for the local authority to claim as a citizen. This is the famous inventor of the Ferguson tractor, affectionately known as 'the wee grey Fergie' with its rear hydraulic lifting arms that revolutionised farming throughout the world, the patent being eventually purchased by Henry Ford. Ferguson is also remembered for building his own aeroplane which he flew at Newcastle, Co Down in 1909.

There are five Moravian churches active to-

day in Northern Ireland: Ballinderry, Kilwarlin (near Moira), the well known village of Gracehill near Ballymena is known as a Moravian settlement, and two churches in Belfast; Cliftonville and University Road. In the past other Moravian churches existed in the immediate Lough Neagh area at Sandy Bay, Glenavy and at Cross Hills. Who are the Moravians and where did the sect originate? The story began in Moravia, now in the Czech Republic, founded by a man called John Hus. They are Protestant claiming to preach commonality, Christian unity and equality among the sexes. The Moravians came to Ireland in 1718 largely led by John Cennick, originally a Quaker who became an Anglican. Befriended by John Wesley, he disagreed with doctrine and eventually became a member of the Moravian church, establishing most of the Northern congregations. There was also a Moravian church in Upper Ballinderry. A house was leased for single ladies and in 1758 it is recorded they were engaged in lace-making and embroidery. Nineteen single brethren were resident in a house quite close by; at this time church membership is recorded at two hundred and five. The history of the congregation records that due to lease problems the single brethren moved to Gracehill while the single sisters decided to move to Gracefield, on the opposite side of the lough near Ballyronan. As the journey by land would have been long and arduous, they travelled by barge across the lough. Half way across the barge sprang a leak and they were forced to throw all their worldly possessions overboard, fortunately by continuous bailing and praying they reached the other shore.

Aghagallon, 'the field of standing stones', a village that is ever increasing in population, lies close to the Lagan canal. Any driver will know it by the artificial chicanes and long humps on the road supposedly to slow the traffic, something the local youth drivers use for their own brand of excitement. This is an area with an unusually high concentration of old churches and graveyards. Aghagallon boasts no less than two, Aghalee one and of course that at Portmore, all within a relatively small area. It is suggested both Aghagallon churches were founded by the same saint, roofed with oak shingles and both destroyed by Cromwell forces. I met a very interesting gentleman at Magheranagaw who helps to keep the graveyard in impeccable order; he showed me a flat stone called the 'Saint's Bed' where allegedly the chattels of the church were hidden before it was destroyed. I gather once there were plans to investigate the theory but the mystery is still unsolved. This is a remarkably small site overwhelmed by grave stones, the little of the remaining walls are heavily clad with ivy. The other old Aghagallon graveyard is perched on what looks to me as possibly the site of a former rath, here too all that remain are the gable walls. All that remains of the Aghalee church are the two heavily smothered ivy clad end walls, sadly the northern section of the old church building is carelessly littered with sods and the inevitable graveyard yew trees now over power the area.

That then is a brief circumnavigation of the lough, with something of most centres of population, large and small, detailed; and, I hope, demonstrating something of the differences between the eastern shore and the west, the north and the south.

Strange place names attract me; one such is the Tunny, a small settlement close to the lough shore. There is a small connecting canal here which links Lough Neagh with Portmore Lough, and I remember the lads from Lough Neagh rescue telling me of navigating this after dark as part of an exercise – I'm told the lifeboat was virtually the same width as the canal!

This area is situated in the Deerpark and was once called the Tunny Park. Tunny Point juts out into the lough and forms the boundary of Lady Bay, possibly named after Lady Conway who presumably dipped her toes in the water here. Here too is a neat little Anglican Church, St Andrew's. There is a lovely man-made harbour here with well manicured grass areas; I recall visiting this spot many years ago for a barbecue, though I understand the area is privately owned.

Close by is Portmore Lough, a shallow haven of tranquillity now managed by the Royal Society for the Protection of Birds. It would be easy to miss this site which would be unfortunate; the little lough is virtually a perfect circle and when there, look for the lapwings now breeding on the marshy shoreland. I like the warden's explanation of how it was formed: he claims a meteor crashed into the area in the dim and distant past, further backing up his theory by citing the myth of Finn McCool throwing the piece of earth that sup-

posedly formed the Isle of Man, suggesting this may have been what the Viking settlers really witnessed! Who am I to cast doubt on such a theory – as he rightly explained, no one has ever challenged his assumption!

Indeed the lough shore is peppered with interesting places special to the locals, who often have their own theory of why the site is special. I would never completely discount local knowledge of the history of an area as this type of knowledge has been handed down through fireside storytelling, sadly television has virtually destroyed this important historical source.

Kieran Clendinning, writing in Craigavon Historical Society's magazine *Review* describes another beauty spot, the townland of Ardmore situated on the Southern shores. He quotes two verses of a rather lengthy poem written in 1905 by a local poet called John McAleese which expresses vividly the intense feeling he had for his home place. Sadly today as a result of modern farming methods the corncrake has gone but the peace and tranquillity of this special place remains for all to appreciate.

T'was in the summer season
In the flowery month of June,
The honey suckle in the hedge
Sends forth its sweet perfume.
The corncrakes in the meadows
And the swallows flying o'er,
All seem to enhance with beauty
My native place Ardmore.

They boast of Scotland's "Bonnie Doon"
But tourist seem to say
Killarney far exceeds it
And so does Killalla Bay
Lurgan is my market town
Where I purchased all my store,
And all these things are but second
To my native place Ardmore.

Traditional Lough Neagh Fishing Boats

The area inspired many poets, two of the best known are 'the poet Haughian' a Montiagh man who lived early in the last century and Moses Teggart from The Birches who was often referred to as 'the poet of the Boglands'. Recently there has been considerable interest in rural poetry and a collection of Teggart's work has been collected by Dr John Wright and published by the South Lough Neagh Regeneration Association. The southern area, east of the River Bann, was rich in colloquialisms and these were recorded in a booklet called *Montiaghisms;* the expressions were collected by the late William Lutton and have been recently republished by the Craigavon Historical Society.

Maghery is a proud historic yet seemingly forgotten area that has suffered from anti-social behaviour in recent years. Now Maghery has a new business park where Holger Lonze, an inspired talented young German, is facilitating a resurgence in traditional boat building – both fishing boats from Lough Neagh and coracles from Donegal and the west of Ireland. The short stretch of canal that served as an entrance to the Blackwater and eventually to the Ulster and Coalisland canals has a fine new bridge awaiting boats from the Erne and Shannon when the Ulster Canal navigation reopens. The Maghery canal replaced an earlier tributary of the River Blackwater and avoided the natural bar at the mouth of the river, always prone to heavy silting from this fast flowing river.

Derrywarragh Island, created by the building of the Maghery Canal, was reputably the scene of an early battle in the eighth century; today the ruins of O'Connor's stronghold stand gaunt against the skyline testifying to the strategic importance of the site protecting intruders from entering the River Blackwater.

Place names around the lough such as the Washing Bay may conjure images of women lining the shore with washboards scrubbing their washing with lifebuoy soap; nothing could be farther from the

O'Connor's strognhold at Derrywarragh

truth. In fact the name is derived from washing in a healing sense as the waters from The Holy River, which flow into the bay, were renowned to have mystic healing properties. The Ordnance Survey Memoirs record the son of a Mr Cunningham being cured of sores over his body in the reign of Charles II. Evidence exists of the area also being known as Fishing Bay; I recall it as a beautiful sandy bay where I paddled as a child on one of those idyllic, balmy sunny days reminiscent of childhood memories, perhaps that is the reason for perfect feet! Local tradition relates the story of Saint Bridget stopping on her way from Kildare to Ardboe and blessing a pool. The rags that hang on a nearby black thorn bush are evidence that it is still frequented today. Brockagh is another name I find rather fascinating and unusual. Situated in Castle Bay the Irish derivation suggests 'the place of badgers'.

The western shores still have numerous interesting buildings scattered around the countryside from the last world war and a particularly impressive castle, Mountjoy built between 1602 and 1605 by the Lord Deputy Charles Blount, the eighth Baron Lord Mountjoy. Built on a low hill with spectacular views across the lough the castle boasts a turbulent history; this is the territory of Hugh O'Neill and the castle was built by the British when O'Neill was forced to retreat prior to the Flight of the Earls. It is reputed that the fort which originally stood on the site was known as Fuath na Gall which I am informed translates to Hatred of Foreigners. That is certainly not true

Roughan Castle

today as this is rural Ulster at its best, where the walker salutes the motorist and the farmer pulls his tractor aside to let the motorist pass.

Historically perhaps the most significant of all adjacent sites is that of Tullaghogue, or Tullyhogue as it is often referred to. This is an area situated some two miles from Cookstown and yet relates significantly with the early history of the western shores. Tullaghogue fort, a relatively short distance from the hamlet bearing the same name, was known as the home of the early kings of Ulster, the place where they were crowned and proclaimed king. I find this a fascinating area, over one thousand years of Irish history depicted within the wide earthen banks; here we can relate the line of his-

tory from Niall of the nine hostages through to Hugh O'Neill and the Flight of the Earls. The area has numerous old graveyards yearning to be rediscovered, all containing evidence to an area steeped in the history of Ulster. Tyrone became a kingdom within Ireland ruled by one of Niall's sons called Eogan, eventually his name altered over the years to become Tyrone. Eogan's descendents became the O'Neill's of Tyrone with their headquarters and the family seat in the town of Dungannon. Their castle was eventually burned by the retreating Hugh O'Neill to prevent it falling to Lord Mountjoy. Tullaghogue fort, with its wooded earthen banks stands in the townland of Doorless. Kings of Durlas, associated with the fort, were recorded as early as the mid 900s, one

Tullaghogue Fort where Kings of Ulster were crowned

of which was drowned close to Ram's Island in 1121; it is easy to see how the name became anglicised to that of today. It is suggested the stone inauguration chair which existed on the mound as late as 1602 was smashed by English forces associated with Mountjoy when he finally captured Hugh O'Neill – that story is told later.

The spectacular star-shaped fort that once stood on the County Armagh bank of the River Blackwater close to the village of Charlemont has sadly disappeared. Mountjoy built this fort in 1602, the fort being called after his Christian name; it housed one hundred and fifty soldiers under the command of Sir Toby Caulfield. There once stood a series of delightful homes here built by members of the Caulfield family who, on being promoted to the peerage, assumed the title of Charlemont. However the really impressive architectural jewel was Roxburgh Castle built on the opposite bank of the Blackwater and modelled on a French chateau. Sadly this magnificent edifice was destroyed by fire around the same time as the house contained within the fort. I came across an advert from the *Portadown Weekly News* of August 13th 1859 where the last remaining materials from the house contained within the fort were auctioned, I wonder does anything remain? The present day gatehouse, once with an impressive drawbridge, dates from the seventeenth century, today passers by look in awe at the grand cast iron gates reputedly made and designed by Richard Turner,

the Dublin-based iron merchant responsible for the design of the conservatories in Kew Gardens, London and that in Botanic Gardens in Belfast.

Counties Antrim and Down were never part of the original plantation of Ulster. Antrim was an attractive settlement area for the lowland Scots, mainly Presbyterians being persecuted in Scotland, thus the originality of the Ulster-Scots language in County Antrim and the local affinity in speech dialect. Antrim is a town that embraces the past with the present; proud of what has gone before yet reaching out, welcoming the unknown that is yet to come, it once saluted the multi-national company of British Enkalon, felt cheated when they hurriedly left, yet readily shook off the after effects and without doubt will progress to better things.

The lough shoreline is littered with ecclesiastical remains, from an ancient church at Oxford Island, the highly decorative high cross of Ardboe and Cranfield old church to a fascinating old graveyard site near Lower Ballinderry known as Laloo. Strangely most historic church sites are small; the remnants of buildings indicate modest structures with unusually small burial grounds. In the book *The Modern Traveller to the Early Irish Church* by Kathleen Hughes and Ann Hamlin, the writers cite the practice in Ireland of rebuilding a church nearer the main centre of population and of abandoning the former building and site and moving to where the people lived. They illustrate this point by describing the settlement at Lower and Upper Ballinderry where the church building has moved three times. Hence the parish name of the church does not necessarily indicate the building is situated within the traditional parish boundary. Headstones in graveyards are a relatively modern phenomena, really dating from the mid seventeenth century. Ireland is particularly rich in early carved stonework, from decorative stones to pillars and the ornately carved high crosses all excellent examples of early Christian art. Notice too the number of circular graveyards, often surrounded by trees, perhaps indicating these were once raths, clan or family settlements most often found on higher ground, settlements that would have been easily defended against attack.

Traditionally early church buildings would have contained items made from precious metals, silver chalices, bowls and communion ware. Often the wealth of an area was reflected in the Christian church but rarely in the lifestyle of the vast majority of the population. One theory for the Irish Round Tower is that it was a refuge for those associated with the church, monks, clergy etc and that this was a place where church valuables could be stored and defended. This is often substantiated by the doorway being some distance up from the ground, entry being by a ladder which could be pulled up inside the tower before the door was slammed closed. Was this the churches' defence against the Viking marauders that plundered early monastic sites around Lough Neagh? I personally find this theory much more acceptable than that of a bell tower – after all why would it be necessary to have a bell tower on Coney or Ram's Island.

There are many theories as to when the Oxford Island site outside Lurgan was last used for public worship; little exists today other than random stones to indicate the exact location of the church and adjoining graveyard though there is a photographic record of the gavel wall. When the Brownlow family came to the area in the early 1600s it was known at least one other church existed in the area, that in Shankill old graveyard in Lurgan. Prior to the Oxford Island site being reformed and created as a nature reserve, a pig farm existed on the site. Indeed the gavel wall of the old church may well have constituted part of the roadway that led to the piggery. I recall locals relating stories of the pigs unearthing human remains while scuffling outdoors. There are numerous burial grounds attributed to localities in this south Lough Neagh area – Dr Frank McCorry has identified one near the late John Emerson's house in Ardmore on the site of the original Ardmore Church and possibly two adjoining Lough Gullion in Derrycorr.

The great Methodist preacher John Wesley made many visits to the Lough Neagh area and on one such visit on Monday 26th April 1762 he called at a terraced house in Lurgan to visit an inventor and watchmaker called William Miller. Miller had invented a talking clock and Wesley recorded in his diary,

'It was the figure of an old man standing in a case with a curtain drawn before him. A clock stood on the other side of the room. Every time the clock struck, the figure opened the door with one hand, drew back the curtain with the other, turned his head as if looking round the company, and then said, with a clear, loud articulate voice; 'Past one, two, three' and so on'.

This phenomenon attracted so much attention that Miller was forced to dismantle it as he had so many callers to view the invention and hence could not attend to his own business. Wesley visited the house again some eleven years later only to be in-

formed by the intrepid inventor that he planned to make two more men, not only to speak but to sing hymns alternately. Wesley's story was verified by other visitors, and I gather Miller wished to sell the invention but had no offers; regrettably the invention remains a mystery to this day.

Anyone who travels up the western shore from the southern end will be familiar with a very bad bend in the road around a church and graveyard; this is the parish church of Clonoe. This beautiful stone built church is one of the oldest church buildings in Northern Ireland on a site that is recorded as far back as the twelfth century though the board outside records the foundation of the church as 1431. Strange names fascinate me. Not far from junction twelve on the motorway is the Toby Hole graveyard, again we must go back into history to find a record of a church; back to the Plantation map of 1609 where there is a record of a roofless church, and one can only assume this is an early site of the present church at Tartaraghan.

The western shores are home to one of the finest high crosses in Ulster and one which ranks among the best preserved in all of Ireland. It is situated on a small hill, the original shoreline of Lough Neagh at Ardboe. I always think of Ardboe in two parts, the hamlet on the main road along the western shores and the settlement close to the edge of the lough where the cross is found. The erection of the cross is attributed to the ninth or tenth century and most likely formed a valuable part of Saint Colman's monastery, a wooden structure built in

Clonoe Parish Church

possibly the sixth century and burned in 1166. I confess to liking the legend describing the building of the monastery; it is said the structure was built with the milk from a cow which came out of Lough Neagh and returned to the lough when the building was complete. On re-entering the waters it is alleged it lowed 'Ard Boe' meaning, 'hill of the cow'. The cross is carved from sandstone, the soft stone having weathered much over the years. There are twenty two panels depicting Biblical scenes including Daniel in the lions den, David slaying Goliath and scenes depicting the crucifixion of Christ. In the north west corner of the graveyard is the dead stump of an old beech tree where coins have been embedded indicating

a prayer for cure from an illness. It is further suggested that any who removes a coin simply transfers the ailment or illness to the perpetrator, hardly a risk worth taking.

When driving up the western shore, I am always struck by the beautiful new chapel as I approach Ardboe. I confess to having written mostly about ecclesiastical remains and have ignored more modern architecture, but this ornate house of worship is indeed impressive by any standards. Elevated, the Stations of the Cross portrayed on the front inspire the word glorification to me; that is surely the statement that any place of worship should make, ultimate worship of our creator. On the

other side of the road, the large well-kept grave-yard in itself makes a declaration; here are a people respectful of the dead, mindful and loving of those that once gave so much love to them. At night the lit candles portray life amongst death, surely this epitomises everything that underlies the Christian faith.

Laloo or Laa Lua graveyard occasionally referred to as Portmore old cemetery lies at the end of a little road from the village of Lower Ballinderry proceeding through fields adjoining the remains of Lord Conway's former castle. Bearing in mind the lowering of the lough, the site would have been an island for months at a time; certainly the surrounding land is boggy and low lying. On a pleasant evening I find this sacred site peaceful

in an idyllic sense, here is a place where you can find your true self. The only sounds to disturb the peace and tranquillity are bird song or the scuffling of an animal in the thick double hedgerow. The undulating ground surface and the remaining ivy clad stone rubble walls conjure sounds of music, of heavenly angelic robed singers praising the Almighty. No unnatural sound seems to disturb the peace of those privileged to be interred in this sacred spot. The church was dedicated to its founder, Saint Lau, who may have been Saint Molua, and in the mists of time a special mass was said on the 4th August each year. The Stations of the Cross were to be found outside the enclosed graveyard, some were denoted by clumps of stones along the waters edge, allegedly still visible today. Make sure you locate the Bullaun Stones, which

Dromore Cathedral where Bishop Jeremy Taylor is buried

are stones hollowed out and possibly used as a baptismal font; allegedly the water has curative properties and allegedly the indentation never dries out.

This would have been the church where the Reverend Jeremy Taylor preached before building and financing the building of the Middle Church, found alongside the road connecting Upper with Lower Ballinderry in 1668. The middle church replaced the pre-reformation building as before the lowering of Lough Neagh the surrounding land may well have flooded, thus access to this lough side site would have proved difficult and inconvenient for Taylor. The Reverend Taylor was a dynamic spiritual leader and renowned author born in 1613 and educated at Cambridge. He served under Archbishop Laud who was at that time Archbishop of Canterbury and eventually became chaplain to King Charles I. After being retired to Wales as a result of falling out of political favour, he was eventually elevated to Bishop of Down and Connor. This invitation to come to Ireland is attributed to Edward Conway whose dwelling adjoined Portmore. Taylor could best be described as a controversial pastor whose relationship with both Presbyterians and Catholics was eventful, though his early death in Lisburn at the age of 54 was more likely as a result of his caring ministry and the tragedy of seeing three sons buried within a relatively short period. His grave may be found in the grounds of Dromore Cathedral.

Abandoned in 1824, the Jacobean styled Middle

The interior of the Middle Church, Ballinderry

Church at Ballinderry is a building in a time warp; its walls, originally white washed, circular windows and the simple interior are a testament to the ideals of Bishop Taylor. The uncomfortable old square backed pews, made of Irish oak, portray warmth against the grey stone slabbed floor, indeed it is suggested much of the wood for the lath plastered ceiling, may well have originated in the old Portmore church. The original three level pulpit domineered the worshippers, dare I suggest making them feel subservient under the ministry of this eloquent speaker. Candles illuminated the building as they do today; the present slated roof replaced the original wooden shingles. The church building is known locally as the 'barn' church, it being similar in structure to the traditional Irish cottage and barn. Relics of the original church survive today, the former communion table and an oak chest still adorn the present Ballinderry Church built in 1824 and the fine coat of arms in the present church may well have originated in Lord Conway's castle. The outside staircase gave access to the gallery and is a newer addition to the building.

Conway's castle, now identified by surrounding stone walls was demolished in 1761. The parklands surrounding the demesne were well stocked with deer, pheasant and other game. This area was once a great oak forest, the area known as Killultagh meaning the great wood of Ulster. Conway's estate was vast, stretching from Derriaghy to the shores of Lough Neagh. The derivation of the name Ballinderry suggested a settlement in the

Cranfield Old Church

oak wood, this has been immortalised in the song *Ballinderry*.

'Tis pretty to be in Ballinderry,
Pretty to be in Aghalee
'Tis prettier to be on bonny Ram's Island
A-sitting forever beneath a tree.

For often I sailed to bonny Ram's Island,
Arm in arm with Phelim, my love.
He would whistle and I would sing,
And we would make the whole island ring.

"I'm going," he said, "from bonny Ram's Island
Out and across the deep blue sea,
And if in your heart you love me, Mary,
Open your arms at last to me."

'Twas pretty to be in Ballinderry
But now it's as sad as sad can be,
For the ship that sailed with Phelim, my love,
Is sunk forever beneath the sea.

Between Toome and Randalstown lies the jewel in the crown of historic church remains, Cranfield Old Church. Again situated on the shores of the lough, this site dates to 130 AD. The area name means 'The Wood of Wild Garlic', and the present church building dates from 1660. The doorway sits low in the bank and the approach reminds me of the abbey building on Devenish in Lough Erne. Pause and gaze through the east window that over-looks the lough and drink in the panorama that lies ahead. This is peace personified; the day I was there I couldn't hear the noise of the distant planes

The Holy Well of Saint Olcan

be amazed at the number of rags hanging on the bushes; rags that bathed and soothed an ailment then hung on the branches and while the material rots so the ailment heals and disappears. The tradition evidently survives and is still very popular today.

taking off from Belfast International Airport even though they were clearly visible soaring into the blue sky, only the distant thud of a sand boat, fully laden, lying low in the water and making her way to one of the sand depots. The site is not dissimilar to Ardboe, the surrounding graves bring a sombre reminder to the fragility of life and those who have found peace and rest here await the coming again of the promised one, the Messiah. Go down the rickety stone steps to the reclaimed shore area and take a left to the Holy Well, once blessed by Saint Olcan; its amber pebbles which are clearly visible are crystals of gypsum. Local tradition claims these pebbles have great healing powers, used by women during child birth, by men to protect them from drowning and even if swallowed they would ensure safe passage for those unfortunate individuals forced to leave their homeland for the New World of America. The visitor will

Parliament. One of the locks on the navigation has already been restored, that at lock twelve opposite the new Lisburn Civic Centre.

The Lagan Canal had two engineers, one who built the Belfast to Sprucefield stretch, and the other, Sprucefield to Lough Neagh. The Belfast to Lisburn stretch is a mixture of river and canal, never the best solution for a navigable waterway. In September 1763 this new navigation was opened as far as Lisburn and the *Lord Hertford,* a sixty ton lighter, made the first voyage, reaching Lisburn. This boat belonged to Thomas Gregg, a prominent Belfast merchant. Between 1763 and 1765 the river was then made navigable as far as Sprucefield and here construction ceased. The original estimate of £20,000 to open the entire canal had proved totally inadequate; indeed by this time nearly twice that amount had been spent. The funds for building the canal were to be raised by levying one penny a gallon on ale and four pennies a gallon on spirits within the wider district of Lisburn, contributions from the Dublin Government and the remainder, the Marquis funded himself.

Sadly today the canal is in three distinct stretches: Belfast to Sprucefield, Sprucefield to Moira and Moira to Lough Neagh. Our enlightened politicians in the middle of the last century built the M1 motorway on the bed of the canal from Sprucefield through to Moira, so the middle stretch has gone. The Lagan Canal is twenty seven miles long with twenty seven locks; eighteen lock-keepers were employed. Most of the lock-keepers had only one lock to look after. Exceptions were the unique flight of four locks, fourteen to seventeen still visible at Sprucefield and a set at Aghalee near Lough Neagh. The lock-keepers lived in a lock house each with a small garden; all were designed so that the lock-keeper could see his lock from virtually any part of the house.

The lock at Stranmillis is now difficult to find. The lock walls can just about be traced in at the edge of the car park, beyond Cutter's Wharf restaurant at Stranmillis. Beside the lock-keeper's house was one of two bank rangers' houses. Naturally enough, both ends of the canal were busy places; tolls had to be collected according to the tonnage of the cargo carried and all had to be entered into a ledger, details included the name of boat, the lighter man's name, the owner of boat, the destination, the draft of lighter, date etc. Interestingly boats were described as lighters in the North of Ireland and barges in the remainder of the country. Many reasons have been proffered; was it because they were lighter in weight?

Picture the early morning scene at daybreak: the horses lined up waiting to be hitched to the barge, then through the lock, and onwards to their destination. Place names en-route are familiar today, Newforge, where the towpath crossed the waterway; Shaw's Bridge, again a change of side for the tow path and on to Edenderry. This is a beautiful tree-lined stretch, popular today with walkers, past the Sir Thomas and Lady Dixon Park and the area

Shaw's Bridge

known now as the Lagan Valley Regional Park.

The lock houses on this stretch were noteworthy; Thomas Omer, being Dutch, brought the continental influence to the lock house design. These two storey houses were very pretty, there is a delightful example to be seen at Drumbridge. Another five locks and Lisburn beckoned. One of the notable features of this section is the high arched, sandstone bridge at Ballyskeagh, known locally as the 'high bridge'; I understand this was used as gallows at the end of the nineteenth century, then came the hamlets of Lambeg and Hilden. This began the region in mid Ulster noted for its linen mills and its bleach greens. Barbour's mill loomed large and was indeed a major customer of the Lagan Navigation Company. The mills used the river water for the bleaching process and perhaps as they had already been established, there was conflict between the two regarding water extractions. Above the canal and behind the factory is Hilden House, a classic Georgian House built as the family home of the Barbour family in the 1820s. The Barbours were noted linen barons and carried on the linen business in the mill which dominated the little hamlet of Hilden. This was by any standards a huge operation, at a time the mill employed over 1500 workers. The factory had its own quay, largely for the delivery of coal, and it also ran its own barges, the most notable being the *Nellie* and the *Eva,* named after two of Barbour's daughters. Barbour's was not the only

The Thomas Omer lock house

mill in the district, other notable linen firms were Richardson Sons and Owden and, of course, the factory run by the Coulston family. Hilden Lock which is just out of sight but beside the old factory is referred to locally as Scott's lock. Lock-keepers who attended the lighters here over the years were McAlice, Smyth and McPoland. Associated with most of the locks on this stretch was a weir, the lock-keepers were also responsible for the mainte-nance and water level at each weir.

On then to the town of Lisburn and the new Island Civic Centre, situated on the island site between the canal and the river. The original factory, locat-ed on the present site of the new Civic Centre, was the Vitriol Factory which eventually became an-

other linen mill known as J. J. Richardson's. The river flows round the back of the Civic Centre and in front is the newly restored cut, or canal section. The new lock gates have been installed at a cost of one million pounds with a set of flood gates at the upper end of the chamber.

Lisburn was without doubt the most important port on the navigation. Its harbour was always a hive of activity. One of the most beautiful vessels to grace its jetties was the *Lord Hertford,* a vessel of sixty tons that plied between Belfast and Lisburn. This barge was the first to make the journey in 1763, effectively opening the new navigation. On that occasion it carried numerous important la-dies and gentlemen who dined on board. We are

told a band played on board throughout the voyage and it was a beautiful sunny day. Alas Lisburn was also the destination of the last barge which came to the island mill site in 1954 with a load of coal. The town had nine quays, one was owned by the navigation company and the other eight were privately owned. The majority of the cargo handled was coal for the adjacent gas works, though other cargoes included linen, corn, flour, timber, farm produce etc. Tolls were charged on cargoes but in 1813 to encourage greater use of the waterway it was decided to waive charges on potatoes, hay and straw moving downstream. It is fair to say one of the aims of building the Lagan Canal was to ensure the port of Belfast would share in the success of the coal exports from the Tyrone coalfields, but like the Newry Canal, more coal was carried upstream than downstream. Freight rates were between 5s and 6s per barge and about 9d per ton, depending on the cargo carried.

Lisburn could also boast a dry dock erected by Henry Mulholland, a timber merchant. It was said to be big enough for two to three lighters at any one time. The last lighter brought there for repair was during the last war, in 1943. The family associated more than any with Lisburn docks was that of the Hanna family. John Hanna was in charge of the quays while his brother James and his son Dick were lock-keepers. Dick gave over sixty years service as a lock-keeper and is reputed to have rescued over twenty people from drowning in the canal, a feat for which he was awarded the Royal Humane Society Award. The navigation

A horse-drawn barge on the Lagan Canal

this many times, I can't dispute the theory as I've never seen a rat steal an egg!

Like so many of the waterways in Northern Ireland the Lagan Navigation found it difficult to compete with road and rail transport. After the outbreak of World War Two, canal traffic began to decline. Competition from the railways and the improved road network were just too much. In 1954 the stretch to Lough Neagh was officially abandoned and in 1958 the stretch from Lisburn to Belfast fell too. Sadly the abandonment went virtually unnoticed by the general public, the rest is history.

The Tyrone navigation or as it is more commonly known, the Coalisland canal, was built between 1733 and1773. The problem of transporting coal from the pits at Drumglass to the newly con-structed basin in Coalisland had still to be solved. Perhaps this problem was to be the most fascinating solution of all. The engineer employed to solve the problem was a Franco-Italian called Davisco de Arcort, known in the locality as Ducart. He proposed building two short stretches of canal and a number of inclined planes or, as they are more commonly known, dry wherries, to transport the coal from the coal fields to the basin in Coalisland. These wherries were a type of railway that carried small two ton boats on cradles; the boats were used on the canal stretches and the cradles on the railway stretches, the idea was the full load was carried down hill while the empty boat on a cradle was carried up hill, assisted by horse power, one counter balancing the other. Needless to say this scheme could never have been described as a roaring success, as from the outset it was dogged with problems.

Hence, by the end of the 18th century, the ports of Newry and Belfast were ideally placed for the exporting of products conveyed to them by the canals. Much discussion ensued as to how best to complete the infrastructure; the need for a water borne link to Lough Erne and eventually the Shannon. Early in the 19th century the engineer John Killaly, employed by the Directors General of Inland Navigation, was directed to investigate the building of a link to the West to open up Fermanagh, Monaghan, Cavan and Donegal and eventually this link into the Shannon. Killaly had gained valuable experience from working on the Royal Canal. His original proposals were to build a navigation with dimensions similar to those he had built on the Royal, though with narrower locks, the narrowest lock on the Royal being 13' 3". The total cost was to be in the region of £223,000, which transpired to be nearly twice the original estimate.

The scheme seemed a strange proposal from someone of the ability of Killaly as the proposed dimensions were not compatible with the other Northern navigations. The new proposals would create a navigation some eighteen inches narrower than the narrowest locks on the Lagan, Tyrone and Newry navigations, thus to build a waterway not compatible with those directly dependent on it seemed a rather foolish proposition.

He also questioned if the water supply of Quigg Lough, situated outside Monaghan, would be adequate for the complete canal, and though he sug-gested deepening it, this was never completed. Thomas Telford was brought over to inspect the plans and costings, but despite much local support the scheme did not see fruition for a further thirteen years. In the meantime financial wrangling put further pressures on the proposals and what was eventually proposed was more like an exercise in cost cutting. Projected returns were based on tonnages carried on the Grand Canal, the most successful of all the Irish navigations, but these figures could never have been achieved by any Northern waterway. The original contract had been given to a contractor named Henry Mullins and McMahon however for whatever reason they withdrew and the contract was eventually awarded to William Dargan, perhaps best known for works associated with the building of railways. Dargan was the main contractor for building the Kibeggan Branch of the Grand Canal. Sad to say Killaly and Telford would not see the fruits of their labours as Killaly died in 1832, followed by Telford a year later. Another notable engineer, William Cubitt, again perhaps also better known for his association with railway building was appointed to progress the scheme to fruition.

The Ulster Canal eventually opened in 1841 and linked the two major expanses of water, Lough Neagh, in the centre of the North, with Lough Erne in the West. The original plan was to create a navigable waterway to link the ports of Belfast, Newry and Coleraine with the West and eventually onwards to the River Shannon, opening up the possibility of passage to Limerick, Dublin

An Ulster Canal bridge showing the towpath

or Waterford. It could be argued the success of the newly opened Ulster Canal depended on the completion of the final Shannon/Erne link, then known as the Ballinamore and Ballyconnell Canal. This canal was built during the famine period and the delay in construction can probably be attributed to the lack of able bodied navvies. The Ballinamore to Ballyconnell waterway was opened to navigation in 1860, alas by the time it opened the Ulster Canal was virtually impassable, having been dogged by a lack of adequate water supplies and the problems associated with the narrow locks. The Ulster canal was then closed for major repairs but by the time it was re-opened the Ballinamore to Ballyconnell Canal had all but

been abandoned. The original Shannon/Erne link had been a complete failure; only nine boats had successfully made the passage, quite a contrast to the phenomenal success of the re-opened waterway today. The improvements carried out to the Ulster Canal did bring a limited increase in traffic to the Ulster but by the turn of the century the canal was again in decline. Thus today, the shoe is on the other foot; to further enhance the success of the Shannon/Erne and to bring tourists into Lough Neagh we need to complete the missing link, we need to re-open the Ulster Canal and we must learn from the failures of the original navigation.

The dry dock at Moy on the Ulster Canal

All the remains of Tynan Abbey

The Ulster canal is forty six miles long with twenty six locks. It left the River Blackwater just below the village of Moy and climbed through nineteen locks to the summit on the far side of Monaghan, descending through seven further locks, a drop of seventy feet, down to the Finn River where it enters Lough Erne near the Quivvy Waters close to Newtownbutler. Shortly after leaving the Blackwater, the canal ascended seven locks, through the Benburb gorge, arguably the most spectacular and scenic, yet the most difficult section in engineering terms and indeed the most costly aspect of the waterway, then on to Middletown. This stretch was one of the most picturesque, journeying through the estates of Lord Caledon, the Stronge estate at Tynan Abbey and skirting the Leslie estate at Glaslough. The rise to Monaghan necessitated the building of seven locks in quite close succession; the canal then skirted the town and headed for the village of Smithborough. Outside Monaghan a feeder was constructed to create a water supply from a small lake known locally as Quigg Lough. The canal then winds its way to Clones through some striking rural countryside before reaching its destination, Upper Lough Erne.

The remaining navigable waterway associated with Lough Neagh is the Lower Bann, the vast majority of which is river with only short canal stretches as-

Boats moored in front of Portglenone Bridge

sociated with the locks. The original rock barrier at Portna, just outside Kilrea caused much concern in the local parish and caused flooding over a wide area; hence the navigable scheme proposed was as much to do with alleviating flooding as it was to accommodate boating traffic. The navigation has remained open since its inception, now managed by Waterways Ireland, and in recent years it has benefited from much needed investment in the form of new jetties above and below the locks and additional signage to ensure safe passage. This is a diverse scenic water trip with open fields and sections where the banks are forested. Other than Toome at the start and Coleraine towards the north, the main settlements are at Portglenone with its fine three arched stone bridge and navigation cut on the eastern side and built on an origi-

nal fording spot on the river and Kilrea a plantation town with the Diamond, a feature in the centre of the town. Here are the falls of Portna and Movangher, without doubt one of the most attractive areas of the river where the town settlement looks down on the waterway. The Lower Bann operates a voluntary code of practice for water skiers, which seems to work reasonably well and a recent addition to the area is a float plane; how that will co-exist with boating interests has yet to be decided.

The northern stretch of the Lower Bann is a deep section; the banks have native trees clinging to the sides and here is one of the most interesting archaeological sites in all of Ireland – Mountsandel. Alleged to be the oldest known example of a

Mesolithic settlement, radio carbon dating has placed the human occupation here around 7000 BC. Evidence uncovered wigwam-shaped houses and numerous flint artefacts. There is also evidence of a fort here which may be the remains of a motte. Coleraine is reached after the last lock on the system at The Cutts where the river cascades to the tidal section of the river that finishes the journey to the sea at Castlerock.

The Hibernia on the way to a new life

For many years a rusting barge hull lay entrenched in the mud along the bank of the Upper River Bann where the M1 Motorway from Belfast to Dungannon crosses the river; this was an original Lough Neagh Lighter named the *Hibernia*. She lay undisturbed for the last forty odd years, used latterly as a fishing platform for local anglers. A good friend of mine Drew Nelson, an ardent knowledgeable local boating enthusiast, had a dream to see this rusted hulk restored to its former glory.

Built in the foundry at Portadown early in the last century, her early years were spent carrying cargoes on the Lower Bann, the Lagan canal and to Coalisland. She was built from sheets of riveted iron as a commercial barge and later modified to become a pleasure craft when she plied the waters of Lough Neagh and the Upper Bann and the numerous other navigable rivers and canals. Eventually the barge was sold to a Portadown family called Crowe. A son Fred, once a councillor on Craigavon Borough Council, recalls his mother entertaining twelve to fourteen guests on board, seated round a solid oak table. Prior to the motorway being built she was moored above the bridge in Portadown but with the building of the M1 motorway a decision was taken to move her below the motorway bridge in case there was insufficient air draft for her to pass under. Here she was anchored, this was the era of 'The Troubles' and

rumours abounded of terrorist groupings meeting within her cabin to plan clandestine incidents. Time reclaims that which is man-made and neglect and nature took control. The hull filled with water and mud, the reeds grew, even trees took root and what was once revered on the waterways became a mud bucket.

Thankfully the life of this ghost-like icon is to have another chance. After a lot of sweat and man hours, ton after ton of glar was removed from the hull, most being removed the hard back-breaking

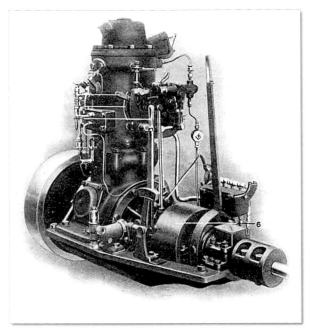

The legendary single cylinder Bolinder engine   89

way, with a shovel. Occasionally there were surprises – the Belfast sink, the Simpson Lawrence toilet and the internal doors made to resemble train carriage doors with their drop down windows, all testified to what was once a grand old lady. As the water was pumped out more of her secrets were revealed, the metal and tiled fireplace and the gaunt old Leyland diesel engine. The original engine had been the legendary Bolinder, a two stroke wonder-working single cylinder diesel that was removed and I gather donated to Lisburn Technical College, I wonder where it is now? Despite the impossible task, the enthusiasm grew, colleagues became inquisitive and some were even prepared to lend a hand. Could this massive resto-

ration project really become a reality? Eventually the barge was towed to the Battery Harbour on the western shoreline where she lay for a winter against the stone wall before being moved the following spring to a scheduled shore near Toome where she was eventually hauled from the water.

Every good story should have a happy ending and this one certainly has; now with the hull repaired and repainted, no less than two diesel engines installed and with a wheelhouse as big as a living room, she is ready for the high seas! Today she lives again, floating in a little cut near Crumlin, a testimony to Drew's vision. The project is now entering the final fit out phase before she re-enters

The Lough Neagh Queen

service for the second century of her life. The plan is to refit the interior, again with luxury living only this time equipped for twenty first century luxury, wood-burning stoves, ensuite bathrooms and a large living area with soft sumptuous seating, look out for the reborn *Hibernia*.

This story of former vessels being reborn is by no means unique, thankfully at present there is a real awakening of our watery heritage and there are numerous such examples of similar projects. Craigavon Museum, ideally situated close to the water's edge and beside the old Lagan Canal terminus at Lurgan, has re-themed as an inland waterways museum and has purchased what I understand to be one of the last examples of a Lagan lighter. She was discovered at one of the sand quays on the eastern shore, neglected forlorn and derelict. The name crudely painted on the bow is

Enterprize however that is not her original name, she was renamed when bought by W. D. Irwin, sand merchants, for use as a sand barge. Reputably she was one of the last barges to come up the canal from Lisburn having been re-bottomed in Browns of Lisburn. At present she has been lifted from the water and stands forlornly in a car park near the Oxford Island museum site awaiting restoration.

Recently I was handed a photograph of the *Lough Neagh Queen,* a vessel which occasionally operated as a passenger vessel on the lough in the early 1900s. She is pictured in Kinnego Cut, the short canal stretch built to bring the lighters and barges to the quay and stores at the end of 'the great road to the lough' now known as the Lough Road, outside Lurgan. Passenger traffic on Lough Neagh was never in that great demand, services were tried on canals with perhaps the most notable being that

on the Newry Canal where a horse-drawn boat operated on a daily basis taking just four hours between Portadown and Newry.

The first recorded steamer on the lough was the *Marchioness of Donegal,* a wooden vessel built in Belfast in 1821 and powered by a 30 horse power Napier engine; she was frequently used to tow barges from Ellis Gut at the entrance to the Lagan Canal to various destinations across the lough. She operated to the mid 1840s proving very expensive to run; eventually the hull was abandoned. The first relatively successful steamer to regularly carry passengers was an iron boat, the first of its type built in Ireland and called *The Countess of Caledon.* Launched in 1838 she was operated by the well known railway engineer William Dargan and ran daily from Vernersbridge on the River Blackwater

to Portadown with the aim of transferring passengers to the railway station in time for the early train to Belfast. It is recorded that on one of her few sojourns to Northern waters, she ran aground near Toome and her captain was flung into the water from where he was rescued by a fishing boat. At a time Dargan actually owned and ran the Ulster Canal and when he retired the service was abandoned.

The Lady of the Lake built in Belfast in 1842 was another of Dargan's passenger boats and it was a wooden paddler that operated between Ballyronan and Lurgan, again to facilitate onward and return train passages to and from Belfast. She operated for a relatively short period and was allegedly sold on to operate on Lough Erne, renamed as the *Countess of Erne.* Dargan replaced her with

The Maid of Antrim

the *Grand Junction,* an iron steamer built in Belfast that was powered by twin 30hp engines, transported to Portadown in sections, reassembled and operated again from Ballyronan but to the railway station in Portadown. Operating to Lurgan often required a lengthy two mile walk to the train station, though on occasion I am informed the service was greeted with horses and traps, whereas the service to Portadown brought passengers to the quay virtually adjacent to the railway station. As with *The Countess of Caledon,* the *Grand Junction* ceased operations when Dargan retired from business life.

Passenger services ceased until the turn of the century though some of the tugs that were used to pull barges across the lough were occasionally chartered for excursions. I mentioned earlier the

photograph of the *Lough Neagh Queen.* She was a twin-screw iron boat, capable of ten knots that had been previously operated on the Clyde as a water bus. She was purchased by a Mr Richard Magee from Toome and operated from various departure points on the lough for about four years. Her elegant tall funnel was hinged so enabling the boat to pass under low bridges.

Perhaps the most elegant of all boats to grace the waters of Lough Neagh was the *Maid of Antrim* again built on the Clyde in 1963, initially ran as the *Scots Guard* on Gairloch and *Holy Loch* operating out of Helensburgh. A Mr Jack Rainey, originally from Larne ran three Maid boats, one operating from Toome, another from Coleraine with Lough Neagh's Maid operating out of Antrim. The three Maids operated with moderate success though unsatisfactory berthing arrangements forced the sale of the three boats. After a short spell in Carnlough the vessel returned to the Clyde where she was again put up for sale. Brothers George and Jim McGarry of the aforementioned boat builders brought the boat back to Lough Neagh, hence began the love affair the local inhabitants have with this classic vessel, a blossoming love affair which initially lasted 32 years and now has again been rekindled. The McGarrys operated the boat all over the lough, including cruises on the Lower Bann. In the 1960s nautical manoeuvres around Ram's Island proved extremely popular corporate outings often calling at the newly erected jetty for barbecues.

Regretfully tragedy struck the McGarry family on the 6th September 1974 when James jnr. was lost over board during a night time cruise. It would take ten long weary days before the lough gave back the body of this promising seventeen year old. The family were determined to carry on and did so with breaks when she was taken to the Foyle for short periods in 1975 and 1976, though it is fair to say the heart was knocked out of the enterprise and in 1977 she was sold to Antrim Council. Thankfully the McGarrys agreed to continue as skippers and other than a two week trip to Belfast Lough coinciding with the visit of the Tall Ships in 1991 she continued to ply the sweet waters of Lough Neagh until 1998.

On the 24th November a few friends of mine decided to attend the auction where the Maid was

Eddie Castles of Derryadd in his traditional clinker-built fishing boat

offered for sale. Con Law, better known as a successful competitor on two wheels, twice winner of the 250cc Isle of Man TT and once at the Ulster Grand Prix and even having raced at Daytona, purchased the vessel and commenced a long and arduous programme of restoration with the plan to re-float this historic vessel and make her once again available for the public to enjoy. Early in 2007, armed with his newly acquired MCA licence for 100 persons, Con is piloting the Maid over the fresh waters of Lough Neagh; what an amazing sight!

There are really only two boats traditional to Lough Neagh, the wooden clinker built fishing boat averaging in length between eighteen and twenty four feet with a beam of seven to eight feet and the Lough Neagh cot, a flat bottomed boat about twelve feet long and three feet across. Common to both boats was the single upright pin on each side

A torpedo platform as it was in 1945

extremely busy wartime base as thousands of aircraft passed through en route to North Africa, the Mediterranean and Europe. It is alleged Langford Lodge was to be a target during Operation Sealion, a planned Nazi invasion of Britain, though thankfully this never materialized. In the early seventeenth century Sir Hercules Langford built a small fishing lodge by the water's edge on the peninsula, which was eventually replaced and a descendent of the family, Sir Hercules Robert Pakenham built the impressive mansion where the family lived until 1940 when the land was sold for the wartime air field development. In 1959 this beautiful house was demolished when the Martin Baker Aircraft Company – the world's largest company manufacturing aircraft ejector seats – purchased the site. More recently, some of the buildings were utilized to display the Ulster Aviation Society's exhibits though these have now been removed and await a new home. Within the grounds of

Langford Lodge is Gartree Church, a delightful building where during the last war the celebrated bandsman Glenn Miller played the organ while entertaining troops stationed at the base.

The names of the other two airfields are today more associated with prisons, Maghaberry and Long Kesh. Maghaberry was to again be a satellite airfield, this time for Long Kesh both acquired by the RAF though mainly utilised by the American forces. Another use for the airfield was as an assembly point for the Stirling bombers manufactured by Short Brothers and Harland in Belfast. Fuselages and wings were constructed in the factory in Belfast and transported by road for assembly in the large hangars. Workers from the Shorts factory were bussed in daily to carry out the assembly work. The Stirling bomber was the first four engined bomber to serve in World War Two. I recall attending motorcycle races there in the 1960s and seem to remember two large hangars which were originally used for Stirling Bombers, as many as 250 to 300 would have been kept at the base. After the war, part of the site became an aircraft scrap yard as it was used as a base to dismantle redundant aircraft. Long Kesh is listed as an RAF base operational from 1941 to 1971 though again largely used by American forces. Perhaps its claim to fame came when during the war effort when King George VI and Queen Elizabeth flew into the air base to encourage all those serving there. Long Kesh played an important role in the planning of the D day landings in Normandy. The plan for the French invasion was to land thousands of

The Halifax which crashed into Portmore Lough

men as secretly and quietly as possible behind enemy lines. Some would parachute in from aircraft and others would be flown in gliders noiselessly dropping to surprise the enemy. The gliders would be towed across the English Channel and released to land at a pre-planned target. Such a manoeuvre required meticulous thorough training, which was affected at Long Kesh, and aircraft simulated the planned operation by towing the gliders across the Irish Sea and jettisoning the glider to land at Long Kesh. These were the heroes of the invasion beaches, Omaha, Sword, Juno, Gold and Utah; this was the highly successful ploy that played such an important part in the allied victory,

In 1971 some of the disused military buildings were used as a detention centre for suspected terrorists; eventually accommodation was provided in the infamous H-blocks and the site renamed the

Maze Prison. The site was also used at that time as a helicopter base, flying reconnaissance missions to the South Down and South Armagh border regions, indeed traffic down the M1 motorway became accustomed to seeing them take off and land regularly. The base was always described as a half finished area, created in an emergency to counter terrorism. Like Langford Lodge, Long Kesh was planned as a possible incursion point for German Paratroopers during the war years.

Portmore Lough, a small virtually circular lake, lies close to Lower Ballinderry a short distance from Lough Neagh. On Christmas Eve in 1944, a young pilot with the Fleet Air Arm took off from Long Kesh airfield in a single seater 'Wildcat' for a practice flight that was to end up as a very lucky escape. Lieutenant Peter Lock was based on the aircraft carrier *Searcher* and while the aircraft were being serviced at Long Kesh the pilots enjoyed a rest while the ship was docked in Belfast for a period of weeks. During their rest they were encouraged by their Commanding Officer to fly practice sorties, practising dive bombing over water. Two planes were on this particular run towards Lough Neagh and just after take off, the second pilot, a chap called Jones, saw flames coming from the engine of his friend's aircraft. Unknown to the unfortunate pilot, the mechanic who had been working on the plane had forgotten to attach a firing line when he replaced the spark plug, hence fuel was leaking. It had exploded causing major damage to both engine and aircraft, indeed increasing the throttle just pumped more fuel on to the

The torpedo platform today, now a bird sanctuary

flames. At eight hundred feet with the wheels up, it was too low to bale out as the parachute may not have opened; the only alternative was to cut the engine and try to glide towards the lough. Fortunately he managed to reach Portmore Lough and the plane belly flopped onto the water, the impact temporarily knocking him unconscious. Eventually Lock came round and scrambled onto the fuselage; he was a non-swimmer and with the water freezing cold he decided to stay put until rescued. A number of locals who had witnessed the incident rowed out in a small boat rescuing the intrepid flyer, it is fair to say he was pretty lucky to even be able to have Christmas dinner that year! Another twist to the story is the rescue

of the plane from Portmore Lough. After the crash it had lain submerged in the shallow water for nigh on forty years when it was rescued by the Ulster Aviation Society and restored. For a number of years it was an exhibit at Langford Lodge museum, sadly that has closed and this lucky exhibit awaits a new venue when once again the public will be given the opportunity to view the aeroplane with the second life!

The lough itself was also a hub of activity; I suppose the most obvious artefact is the remains of the torpedo platform in Antrim Bay. This was constructed in 1942 and used to test fire torpedoes manufactured in Antrim. The structure now resembles a flat platform, but during the war years supported extensive buildings, now it is home to the largest colony of around fifty breeding terns. The McGarry family who resided on the lough shore established Ardmore Boat yard in 1927. They were also very familiar with the lough as they had been fishing for quite some time. As boat builders, they were frequently employed by the Air Ministry to lay practice targets for bombing and aircraft gun practice on the lough. The late Jim McGarry, a man I was privileged to know, one time skipper of the *Maid of Antrim* and fountain of knowledge on the lough has written a fascinating paper describing the activities of legendary aircraft such as the *Vickers Vimy,* the *Hanley Page Heyford* perhaps better known as *The Flying Hayshed.* Jim describes as a boy in the mid-1930s watching the antics of the pilots as they flew low, waving at the stand-up gunner complete with leather helmet and trying to keep apace with the aircraft as he pedalled along the country lanes on his bicycle.

Prior to the outbreak of war, target practice was leisurely and relaxed but as the British forces monitored the build up of the European war machine, so too did McGarry's preparation move up a gear. Initially the family maintained moorings at Langford Lodge and at Killadeas on Lower Lough Erne. Mostly bombing practice was with dummy drops which exploded with a muffled sound emitting a burst of white smoke; when the real thing was used locals on either shore complained of broken and cracked window panes. Eventually to the dismay of local fishermen, a rectangular

area some five miles by fifteen in the lough centre was cordoned off as a practice area. There was a Sunderland flying boat base in Sandy Bay adjacent to Ram's Island where twelve of these aircraft were moored with associated marine craft. In 1944 the huge American Coronado seaplanes flew regular daily sorties between New York and Sandy Bay bringing in troops and supplies for the D day landings. Can't you just visualise and imagine the announcement that could have been made for those flight arrivals! Sadly there were mishaps, usually the crews on water-based ones survived, that was not always the case on land.

The McGarry family built many fine cruisers over the years; a good friend of mine owned a magnificent example named *Mayfly* once based in Strangford Lough, sailing regularly to the Isle of Man and often cruising the west coast of Scotland; her skipper would testify to her excellent sea keeping qualities. Their reputation for quality workmanship and finish spread throughout the boating world and they constructed numerous examples of fine ships, many constructed to order. In the late fifties the McGarrys designed the Ulster boat famous for its agility as a sailing boat. Perhaps the staple product was the well known Lough Neagh fishing boat, their order book always included examples for all areas of the lough. Alas with the introduction of glass fibre boats, the market for wooden boats declined and the brothers were forced to diversify, at which stage they purchased the Maid of Antrim. Many in the boating fraternity today aspire to owning one of the McGarry

*The McGarry brothers
during the last war*

boats, as they are icons of quality of a bygone era, though sadly the downside of owning any wooden old lady are the high maintenance costs. There are few people today prepared to give these vessels the number of coats of varnish necessary to keep the wood of these magnificent vessels in pristine condition.

Pumping sand out of the hold

*An eel cage, which, when submerged,
is used to keep the eels alive*

three hundred people, certainly if the decline isn't halted, livelihoods are in jeopardy. Recently the co-operative have purchased elvers in an effort to halt the decline, perhaps even more drastic measures will be required to reverse the trend.

Fishing on the lough was setting lines to catch eels and nets to catch pollan. The eel lines were huge – anything from two miles to six miles in length, each had a branch line every four or five yards or metres, whichever measurement takes your fancy, and these short lines contained the baited hooks. The bait used was generally worms or small pieces of fish, usually tench or pollan. A line could contain anywhere between one and two thousand hooks, once made of cotton, now the synthetic variety is nylon based. Originally lines would have been set late in the evening or before sunrise, the wife often helping to prepare the line the previous evening, and then the line in its box was steeped overnight to make it more pliable. Catches were limited to forty stone which approximates to two hundred and fifty kilos per week and when the lines were lifted the line was cut leaving the hook in the jaw and the live eel put in a barrel and brought ashore. There they were transferred to a wooden framed wire net cage which was submerged in the lough awaiting the arrival of the lorry with its oxygenated tanks to transfer the fresh product to the Toome eel fishery.

I remember setting a short line one evening with

some friends about a mile away from where we kept the boat and close to a stony bottomed shore. Next day the weather was foul, windy and wet, and as the day progressed the weather worsened. The decision was taken: the line had to be lifted, the engine was fired and off we set. The weather was appalling, on the way to where the line was set, the boat met the waves head on, up and down, up and down, with the rain spiking into our faces. The line was dangerously close to the shore and as we endeavoured to retrieve it the boat was being driven ever close to the stony shoreline. A decision was taken to expedite the procedure we wouldn't bother cutting the line with the hooks and putting the slimy wriggling snake like eels into the barrel, no we would let the lot lie in the bottom of the boat until we reached base, after all due to the heavy rain there was already considerable water in the bottom of the boat. With what limited skill we possessed, we managed to keep enough water under the hull and not run aground, lifted the catch and headed for base. As in all good stories, the weather deteriorated, the swell seemed mountainous, we couldn't see where we were heading, and suddenly we, or was it just me, felt apprehensive. Heading in the agreed general direction, the boat seemed to be lying lower and lower in the water. Goretex jackets hadn't been discovered in those far off days, so the anoraks we wore became saturated.

Progress was painfully slow, now we were standing in a considerable depth of water lying in the bottom of the boat so we decided I should start baling. With a bucket I frantically tried to lower the rising water levels, but when you lean over, the trousers go down and the shirt creeps up and the water then penetrates down the inside of the trouser leg. On and on, it seemed for ever until we saw the familiar shoreline ahead, the boat slipping lower and lower in the water, the speed ever decreasing until eventually we made the incision in the shoreline that was our extremely welcome harbour. Quickly we transferred the eels to the barrel on a trailer behind the car, jammed the crude lid on the top, secured everything as best we could and headed home. To say we were drenched, even wet to the skin was a total understatement, of course we decided there and then that was the end of the line for boating; the boat was to be sold.

Next day dawned bright and clear and we headed back to rediscover the mess we had left the previous evening, what a calamitous site awaited us, the boat was full of water and resting on the bottom! We baled and baled the oily water, no ecological worries then, and eventually got her raised off the bottom, but water seemed to be defeating our efforts, and it wasn't raining. It was then we discovered a butterfly stemmed tap located in the bottom of the boat. When the eels were swimming about in the bottom of the boat, the tap had got turned, hence the reason for the boat slowly sinking. We drained the engine oil, disposed of it in a more environmentally manner, filled the petrol tank with fresh fuel and hey presto, the engine fired into life. The day was idyllic, weather flat calm. Did we sell the boat? Well I'll leave the conclusion of that

Hand cut and dried osiers stacked for basket making at Ballinderry

story to your own imagination!

While there were other forms of line fishing, the cotton draft net was the main means for catching pollan. This is a poke-shaped bag in the region of one hundred yards or metres in length and each opening in the net about two centimetres or just less than an inch. I vividly recall these drying while strung between stakes, the sight along all the lough shores was so common place, especially along the southern, eastern and western shorelines. There was considerable skill involved in releasing these nets into the water, weighted with stones to ensure they trawled the muddy bottom, the boat was anchored and the net hauled in over the stern, such fishing was usually carried out in favourable winter weather and in the spring. Pollan, sometimes referred to as the fresh water herring, were often sold locally around the doors on a Thursday evening, Friday being a non meat day for many, especially Roman Catholics. Pollan

were also exported to some of the bigger English cities, especially London, Liverpool, Manchester and Birmingham. More recently eels are caught with draft nets, let's face it nobody wants the hassle of setting a traditional eel line any more, look for the easier more profitable option.

Migrating eels are captured at weirs on the Lower Bann River at Toome, where the river leaves Lough Neagh; this is managed by the Lough Neagh Fishermen's Co operative. The scale fishery rights on the Lower Bann and of its tributary rivers belong to 'The Honourable the Irish Society', a four hundred year old organisation which leases the rights to Bann systems, a wholly owned subsidiary company, who in turn lease the rights to local angling clubs. The eel fishing rights belong to the Lough Neagh Fishermen's Co operative Society that is as far as The Cutts, an area just south of Coleraine. The Department of Culture, Arts and Leisure is responsible for coarse fishing

A pile of turf

October on their journey to the spawning beds in the tributary rivers. Coarse fishing on the river is an extremely popular sporting activity, the Department of Culture, Arts and Leisure operate two fish farms, and a third one at Portna is privately owned.

The lough shore has always supported numerous cottage industries, one of which is basket weaving. Recently I attended a craft and food fair at Ballyronan where I was fascinated to see the vast range of traditional cottage industries alive and well. Traditional baskets were used for potato gathering, the collection of eggs, holding logs by the fireside and the ever popular ladies' shopping basket. Today diversification ensures craft makers seek new uses for this intricate, beautiful creation. The damp boggy shoreline suited the cultivation of the raw material, osiers commonly known as sallys, but the experts knew the best variety to grow, the ones that would bend and not crack, those that could be woven to create a quality product. Today those involved with the craft are keeping alive a traditional cottage industry, but once it gave much needed seasonal employment to fishermen and other casual workers in small factories. Product diversification was always sought – caged covers for whiskey flagons, hamper baskets, indeed anything was considered, the potato basket however was always the main stay product.

Another lough shore based product was turf or peat found plentifully in the southern shores, formerly a much sought after fuel source and today

in the three canal sections of the river. Are you confused? Well you have every right to be, I am, though I am assured it all works just as a well oiled wheel. The young elvers enter the estuary in autumn and travel upstream aided by special ladders strategically placed at the weirs. Salmon are also present in the river ascending between May and

Dug out turf bogs showing bog cotton growing profusely

desired by gardeners to enrich soils. There were two main types; mud turf, a harder longer burning fuel and cut turf, which was dug from the turf bank. The South Lough Neagh wetlands provide a rich proliferation of peat deposits, formed as a result of decaying plant life over the last ten thousand years. Peat is formed when partially decomposed plants accumulate on top of one another in a water logged environment. Peat sustains unique eco-systems where the main plant life is sphagnum moss, dependent for its nutrients from the water-logged base. Bog land is by its very nature acidic and yet supports rich insect life, sedges and low growing heather type shrubs. Bog wood is a common find during turf excavation, known locally as 'fir'. After the last ice of the Pleistocene period melted, Ireland became covered by dense forest which was mainly composed of oak and fir

trees. The bog eventually overcame the trees and the water logged turf preserved the wood, only to be rediscovered during the subsequent digging for turf.

Mud turf was excavated low down the bank or dug from a water logged trench known locally as a turf drain. The turf was 'tramped' in the drain with bare feet, squeezing the air out making a dense medium. This was a job for warmer weather, trousers rolled as high as possible and hours upon hours of treading, then the wet turf was lifted using a long bladed turf spade and deposited on the raised bank and left to dry. Mud turf burned longer and gave better heat, but because its production was so much more labour intensive, it sold for a higher price. Marketing was usually done on a Friday night, around the doors with a horse and

A farm cart

cart. There were regular disputes, the turf man was always being accused of packing the bag in a way that the bag seemed full, yet had the minimum turf content, and bags of fir could also be bought, great for kindling newly laid fires. Large tree trunks taken from the bog were sometimes sawn into roof purloins or roof trusses for cottages, re-covered logs were turned into furniture, looms, even milk churns. Most farmers owned a portion of moss, one to two weeks intensive footing was required to create an adequate supply for a home for the winter months, and then the material had to dry out before being transported home to be stacked by the gable wall for winter fuel. Moses Teggart, the Poet of the Boglands wrote this poem called *The Turf Cutter.*

*My back is not too stiff to stoop
To work - no matter what;
So I'll clane out the cow-house groop
While you are doin' that.*

*Oh, no! I'm not the laste bit cross, -
But now when labour's throng,
The turf bank I've pared up the moss,
Will crack if left too long.*

*Now get your old Glengarry cap, -
The sun's so hot the day,
Most boys would rather peg a tap
Than fork wet fams away.*

*Put in the fut boards, graip an' all,
The turf-spade, too, I'll wheel;
From your wee showlder should it fall
It might chip off a heel.*

*Coal miners at Drumglass
outside Coalisland*

Wi' sods filled up its every pit
That deep last winter showed,
This ramper - since they gravelled it,
Is like a country road.

That corn is showin' a fine braird!
These early sprouts'll do!
An' here's the bank that I have pared,
An' shovelled smoothly, too.

Wheest! There's our friend the mosscreeper,
Untouched by cant or care,
Och, how the lark-like notes of her
Make sweet the throbbin' air.

These katty turf in the tap graft -
So tough, fill me with the hope,
The bottom ones, if not too saft,
Will cut like yellow soap.

Ye might as well cut through a rug,
Or grazin' closely clipped!
My fut, just now, off the spade lug
Wi' heavy pouncin' slipped.

Wheel these ones out - but not too far, -
That heather height'll do!
(Those bells of ling - how sweet they are!
How fresh an' rosy, too!)

You do not like to cover them
Wi' wet turf or wi'dhry?
Go on! An' think how many a gem
Gets hidden from the eye.

Think, too, of the cowld winter nights,
The fine warm fireside,
The shadows and the shinin' lights
No book from you can hide.

119

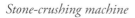
Stone-crushing machine

If I could cut down to the clay
Through buried sprig an' bell,
My summer labour would repay
Me in the winter, well.

But for the brown moss water here,
There isn't half a fall!
Indeed, that march this many a year
Is no march dhrain at all.

When in the hole that lump of bog
Fell with a sudden splash,
How fast the sickly yellow frog
For safety made a dash!

Ah! Hese are fine ones! From the spade,
How smooth an' clane they slip!
Take care! The turf-graip wasn't made
Their shinin' sides to rip.

Dear me! How long that skylark sings!
He's surely in good tune!
No dinner-bell his wifie rings,
An' yet it must be noon.

Wheest! Isn't yon your mother's 'hoagh'?
The mugs are on the shelf!
Run on, my boy, an' I'll bring Coagh -
The craythur, home, myself.

Fine new jetties at Ballyronan

while his three companions were rescued after three and a half hours in the water, David was lost. Determined that something good should come from this terrible tragedy, his father and others raised sufficient funds to purchase a rigid inflatable lifeboat which was named Bungy in memory of David. The volunteer crew trained tirelessly and all too soon it became apparent that one boat based on the southern shores could not provide adequate cover for the entire lough, hence a second boat was purchased and based at the Battery Harbour on the western shoreline, this boat was called the *David Gray*, a tribute to the father who had worked tirelessly to assemble the funding for the enhanced rescue service. The Maritime and Coastguard Agency, with air support provided by Irish rescue helicopters based in Sligo and Dublin, now co-ordinate rescue on the lough providing a professional service required for this new millennium.

While the entrance to Antrim boat club is from the Randalstown road, the club is located where the river called the Six Mile Water enters Lough Neagh at the northern end of the lough. The jetties are located along the western bank of the river fronting a forested area and generate interest for those who frequent the Lough Shore Park, accessed from the town, out past the Recreational Forum and the golf course. Sailing and smaller motor boats now dominate the membership, this is a vibrant club determined to move forward and make it attractive to new members. The new Civic marina planned for the lough shore park may well

spoil the view for those who sit in cars reflecting and staring out over the lough but it should complement membership of the boat club.

Wild fowling has always attracted a sizeable following around the shores evidenced by the sconces or hides built out in the water to camouflage the shooter. There are numerous gun clubs which have purchased or lease shooting rights from the Shaftesbury estates or from local shore land owners. Many of these clubs see themselves as conservationists, feeding and encouraging the young wild life. I will be unpopular with many in stating I have a real problem with this approach as it seems to me they are feeding the young to blow their brains out in adulthood! The mallard duck, like so much of the bird life, is an innocent soul, squawking around as they plunder for food in the mud, easy prey either in water or in that quick flapping winged flight. I understand the need to cull or curtail certain bird population growth; perhaps this revulsion is a throwback to my youth when inadvertently I shot a robin, a regret I still live with.

In 1999 the Lough Neagh partnership was set up to disseminate funds to improve infrastructure around the lough. It has organised numerous successful events to raise the profile of the shoreline. One such event was a medieval fare organised over a weekend in the demesne of Lord O'Neill which brought outdoor drama, extreme sports, equestrian events and promoted local crafts to a province-wide audience. Those privileged to attend were able to view the remains of the castle and the dungeons and to reflect on the halcyon

Shane's Castle, Antrim, showing Camelia House

days when his Lordship ran the little steam railway that brought children and those not so young on a magical journey from the gate lodge to virtually the water's edge. The gaunt ruined castle with its towers, canons, terraces and underground passages is truly atmospheric, conjuring thoughts of joisting knights in armour to medieval banquets with roaring fires keeping the cold lough winds at bay. The castle was burned in 1816, but the ruins, although best viewed from the lough, are truly awesome, definitely on anyone's must see agenda. The history of the O'Neill family, the oldest traceable family in Europe is so closely linked to the history of Ireland. The family still live, work and manage the estate and the present Lord is an approachable, affable gentleman who is generous and very much part of the local community where he works and lives.

Another important publication sponsored and promoted by the partnership is the Lough Shore Trail. As its name suggests, this booklet details a range of trips for the serious and not so adventurous cyclist. I like its introduction where it states, *'more roads, fewer cars'* that certainly epitomises my vision of the minor roads along the western shoreline, where every corner affords a different panorama, from the patchwork like fields to what was once a traditional cottage to the distant shimmering waters of the lough. This is fairy and leprechaun territory, where blackthorn bushes remain untouched for centuries and where superstition rules eternal. I say this respectfully, not in any mocking sense, for those who populate this area are an honourable, respectful, shy and diligent people. This booklet details sites to see, places to visit and most importantly, somewhere to lay the weary body af-

The whooper swan

churches and adjoining graveyards reveal much of what has been hidden for centuries.

ter drinking the pure fresh clean air, washed by the Sperrin mountains on its way east. I confess also to liking the section on hidden attractions directing the inquisitive visitor to quirky destinations as well as the more popular touristy type. Like the western shore, the eastern shoreline has much to offer, again please stray from the main road to the minor ones, go down the grassy pathways, all will be revealed, depending on the season, wild flowers abound, the cuckoo still cries and the sunsets are magical. Winter sees the whooper swan migrate from Iceland to the wetland habitats so popular year after year; the waters too depending on the season host their visitors, in spring watch for the courtship dance of the Great Crested Grebe, a truly memorable sight. Stray a little inland to the villages and settlements, look for the many circles of trees depicting ancient raths, where once family clans lived and defended the local area, the

The Lough Neagh Advisory Committee was set up in 1994 to offer advice on the conservation of the natural and man-made heritage, drainage and navigation and on the management and sustainable development of land and water based recreation, they make recommendations to government and to local authorities. They have made an amazing start to developing facilities around the shoreline through the Lough Neagh Partnership which they set up in 2003 to deliver a £3.2 million pound fund aiming to regenerate shore-based schemes and to promote and market what the lough has to offer. This has been a hugely successful initiative and many local authorities, private individuals and companies have developed infrastructures around the shores for the benefit of tourist and local alike. The scheme has focused on protecting and raising the awareness of environmental issues and the complex bio-diversity of the Lough Neagh basin. The Advisory Committee secured funding for a bio-diversity officer who has raised the profile of the wetlands on to an international stage highlighting issues such as the whooper swans that over winter here returning to Iceland for the summer. With additional powers and finance being devolved to local authorities, future funding will be administered by groupings known as LAGS, three of which will border the shoreline.

It is fair to say the development of water-based tourism is hampered by the lack of a navigation authority to manage the lough. In the west of the province Waterways Ireland, the cross border body set up under the Good Friday agreement, manages the Erne system, the Shannon Erne Waterway and the Shannon river along with the Grand and Royal canals. Also within their brief is the Lower Bann navigation, hence we have the dilemma where bye laws could be introduced for the Lower Bann whereas the largest stretch of water has totally inadequate marking and no authority to ensure safe boating. Indeed it has been suggested that it is irresponsible to promote water-based activities on the lough without proper regulations and enforcement. It is fair to say boat hire, and indeed tourist fishing, has never been developed to its full potential; certainly there is no comparison to water-based activity such as that found on the Erne. The public never cease to be surprised when they realise the bed and soil are in private ownership, perhaps this fact hinders progress as every facility created would be expected to pay a tax to the Shaftesbury estates. There are small areas where the rights have been purchased; Kinnego Bay is an excellent example. The harbour master, with the support of the local council, has singularly created a facility that would equate with any in Ireland or beyond. Restrictions placed on dredging and the need to remove spoil to land fill sites further restrict development.

*Paddy Prunty, Harbourmaster
at Oxford Island*

The late Jim McGarry, often referred to as 'Mr. Lough Neagh', advocated the creation of islands throughout the lough; he suggested these could be used as bird breeding grounds, bird sanctuaries and with jetties which would be a safe haven for boats. They could be quite easily created in shallower places by depositing the spoil from dredging the river mouths, which should satisfy those who are insistent dredged material be either removed or simply moved. Without doubt this is a very big stretch of water and the thought of promoting hire boat activity on such a vast expanse of water needs consideration, but then Lower Lough Erne, Lough Ree and Lough Derg are also large water expanses; they successfully accommodate the hire boat industry and the prosperity generated in those areas is impressive by any standards.

I gather new tourism signature projects are being examined and considered, niche activities, walking, fishing, cycling are a few examples. Surely the Lough Neagh shoreline is ideally placed for the development of such nodes, the Lough Neagh cycle trail established by the Partnership is one such example. Boating shouldn't just be seen as cruisers; canoes, wind surfing are examples of other aspects of boating which require marketing and development. Farm diversification is the buzz word today, what better way to supplement the incomes of small farmers than to create a need for low-cost bed and breakfast accommodation, restaurants, cycle hire, boat hire etc.

Perhaps the greatest future challenge of all is the threat of global warming with the inextricably linked rise in CO2 levels; we must face the risk of what that means for communities around the lough, for the wetlands and for the flora and fauna native to the area. There are so many imponderables to the possible scenario that may or may not happen, in the short term, medium term and long term. The short term may be interpreted as the next ten years, medium as fifty years and long term as the end of the century. One thing that can be stated for certain is the fact that this change is already happening, the evidence exists. Older lough shore residents recall the big freezes that happened in the past when the lough was frozen, when horses and carts were driven across the ice and when the locals skated for weeks on end. My father told me of snow falls of ten feet or two metres deep, gracious today if we have a severe night's frost or a smattering of snow, it causes total havoc for commuters next morning. What can we expect? Well the experts tell us our weather will be warmer, wetter and windier, unusual storms will become more prevalent, summer deluges will be more commonplace resulting in localised flooding. Regrettably due to lack of investment and monitoring, our present sewage treatment infrastructure requires serious investment to enable it to cope with unusual weather systems. Storm water clogs up water courses, gets into storm water overflows and ends up in sewage treatment works where due to unusual high volumes, sewage is allowed to escape untreated. Common sense to me would suggest water extraction should take place in the chain before sewage effluent is released; discharges should always be where the effluent is dispersed to the outlet and hence to the sea.

Without doubt, proposals to build an incinerator outside Crumlin will have a detrimental visual and possibly an odour effect on this immediate area. This plant would generate electricity by burning farm effluent; there is certainly growing opposition to the proposal in the immediate area, understandably from a 'not in my back yard' syndrome. In this era of declining oil-based resources, alternatives need to be considered but there is generally a high environmental price, there is always a delicate balance which someone must determine.

The rise of carbon dioxide gases into our atmosphere will affect the future viability of crop production; it has been suggested that the growing of Ireland's staple crop, the potato, will be severely curtailed, yet wheat could well become a more profit generating alternative. Will the rise in water temperature have an effect on fish stocks; indeed will the native species be able to survive? Will climate change have an effect on the bird and animal species, already birds only found in North Africa have appeared in southern areas of Ireland, certainly we are seeing more and more southern species of fish and mammals around our shores. Of course there is a positive side to climate change, people will want to get out and about more, Mediterranean destinations may well become too hot for holidaymakers and more will choose to spend their vacations at home, hence the need for more tourist related infrastructure and job creation. Summer water levels will without doubt be

Zebra mussels

lower in the future, at least in the dryer seasons, less water could well mean more pollution; what we certainly need is for the government to take this matter seriously and act now to moderate any possible negative outcomes.

Another threat to our bio diversity is the spread of invasive species, non native varieties of plants, animals and aquatic life that now colonise land, hedgerows and fresh water lakes, islands being particularly vulnerable. Perhaps some of the most common plants are giant hog weed, rhododendron and Himalayan Balsam. The grey squirrel and the New Zealand flat worm are both spreading at an alarming rate and the main threat to our fresh water lakes is from zebra mussels. Zebra mussels were first discovered in Ireland in 1994 on the River Shannon and relatively recently have been discovered in Lough Neagh. They are found clinging to hard material and often colonise on the

bottoms of boats, live two to three years and rapidly increase their numbers by releasing millions of microscopic young; weak creatures that rapidly spread in river flows. Their phenomenal spread throughout the Erne system meant it was virtually inevitable that they would spread to Lough Neagh. They filter the water removing plankton which fish feed on and in simplified terms, the water becomes clearer, hence the light penetrates deeper, and in the phosphate enriched waters weed growth is much more vigorous. The implications for the traditional fish population and the fact it is the main source of drinking water aren't really fully understood; the lough is relatively shallow and with it being heavily polluted this is a particularly worrying trend.

Invasive plant species such as Himalayan balsam are now quite common along river banks and shorelines. Again the introduction is relatively

Himalayan Balsam

recent though it is rapidly becoming a real nuisance and is having a damaging effect on native vegetation. It grows up to two metres tall, produces a large number of flowers of various shades of pink and purple and is a member of the Busy Lizzie family. When the plant is mature and dry, the slightest movement makes the seed pods explode dispersing the seeds over a wide area from the parent plant – it is estimated each plant produces in the region of two thousand five hundred seeds. The plant that certainly scares me is the giant hog weed, a mighty plant by any reckoning that can grow up to three to five metres tall or in old fashioned measurement, ten to fifteen feet. An unlikely member of the parsley and carrot family its tall tube like hollow stem culminates in coarse toothed leaves and produces a flat topped umbrella like cluster of fine white flowers. Like so many of these dreaded invaders it spreads rapidly, each plant producing up to fifty thousand seeds, ground cover is particularly dense thus eradicating native plants. When touched the poisonous sap reacts with the skin and subsequent exposure causes the skin to burn and after some fifteen to twenty hours after contact, produces large watery blisters that could eventually cause recurrent dermatitis.

The plight of our native red squirrel has been well documented; it was originally thought these were being killed by the intruding grey, now it is felt the grey simply destroys the habitat of the red by consuming vast amounts of the food once reserved for its native red cousin. Of perhaps even greater

A cheeky visitor to our shores!

consequence though less well known, is the spread of the New Zealand flat worm. Turn up any pot sitting in your garden and it is highly likely one of these is lurking below, wriggling frantically when disturbed. These are flat mucus covered dark purplish coloured creatures with pointed ends that stay close to the surface, their exclusive diet consisting of our native garden worm. The eggs are shaped like a shiny black capsule and each egg produces in the region of two to ten off spring. When an earthworm is located, it smothers it in this mucus which in effect is the digestive juice and is then sucked and consumed, the diet being in the region of one to two every week. When the food supply is exhausted, it has the ability to shrink and wait anything up to two years. Scary stuff all this alien invasion of our native space!

Thankfully today there is a real resurgence in interest in canals, this time around for leisure use.

A delightful lock-keeper's cottage on the Ulster Canal

The popularity of both the Lagan and Newry canal towpaths for leisure use has again focused attention on what once was a vital part of our economy. Today the emphasis is on leisure, the exciting new industry which can be the wealth creator. Steps are already under way to re-open the Lagan navigation; the four local authorities, Belfast, Castlereagh, Lisburn and Craigavon have joined together to form a trust to take forward the re-opening of this historic waterway. Plans already exist to re-open the first three locks enabling navigation as far as Shaw's Bridge. With the re-opening of the old lock twelve at Lisburn in front of their beautiful new Civic Centre and the possible re-instatement of locks ten and eleven, naviga-

tion would be enabled on this middle section. The stretch from Moira to Lough Neagh is relatively easy to re-open; dredging of the channel with the re-instatement of lock gates and lock refurbishment would be a fairly inexpensive operation.

With the commencement of the re-opening of the Ulster Canal announced, this will enable cruiser fleets from the Erne and Shannon to come to Lough Neagh and with the re-instatement of the Lagan, Newry and Coalisland canals this could be a mecca for tourist development. The Republic of Ireland has many inland water areas designated as blue flag sites, why none in Northern Ireland? Regarding ownership of the bed and soil of Lough

Neagh, should the Government be bringing this immensely important resource into public ownership so that the fragile ecology is protected for future generations? Leisure facilities need to be managed in a coherent joined up manner and water quality needs serious action, not in the future but now. We all await the day when the Lough will truly be able to take its rightful place as a European tourist icon.